RESTORATION
in the VALLEY

A PSYCHOLOGICAL RESOURCE MANUAL FOR CLERGY

VALINDA M. BOWENS, PSY. D.

RESTORATION IN THE VALLEY: A PSYCHOLOGICAL RESOURCE MANUAL FOR CLERGY.

Copyright © 2017 by Valinda M. Bowens, Psy.D. All rights reserved.

Books may be purchased by contacting the publisher and author at:

SEP Publishing
80 W. Sierra Madre Blvd., #337
Sierra Madre, CA 91024

Connect@DrValindaB.com

Cover Design: SEP Publishing

Publisher: SEP Publishing

Editor: Lee Ann with Book Editing Services

Library of Congress Catalog Number: 2017905491

ISBN: 978-0-9888451-0-7

1. Mental Health 2. Clergy 4. Religious Coping 3. Spirituality

4. Self Help 5. Church Leadership

First Edition

Printed in the United States of America

No part of this book may be reproduced in any written, electronic, recording, or photocopying without written permission of the publisher or author. The exception would be in the case of brief quotations embodied in critical articles or reviews, and pages where permission is specifically granted by the publisher or author.

Although the author and publisher have made every effort to ensure that the information in this book was correct at press time, the author, publisher, and editor do not assume and hereby disclaim any responsibility or liability to any party for any loss, damage, or disruption caused by errors or omissions, whether such errors or omissions result from negligence, accident, or any other cause. There are no representations or warranties, express or implied, about the completeness, accuracy, reliability, or suitability of information contained in this book. Any use of this information is at your own risk.

This book is not intended as a substitute for the medical advice of licensed physicians and/or mental health therapists.

You should regularly consult a physician in matters relating to your health, and particularly with respect to any symptoms that may require diagnosis or medical attention.

The author of this book is not an attorney. The information contained in this book should not be construed as legal advice. The suggestions, recommendations, and processes discussed herein are not a substitute for consulting with an attorney. You should consult with a licensed attorney to the extent you have a specific legal issue related to topics discussed in this book.

DEDICATION

Now unto him, who is able to keep you from falling, and to present you faultless before the presence of his glory with exceeding great joy. To the only wise God our Savior, be glory and majesty, dominion and power, both now and forever. Amen.

For inspiration: My pastor, Rev. Rodney J. Howard Sr.

For guidance: My minister, Rev. Gerald Bailey

For unconditional love and support: My mother, Viola J. McGlover

For provision: My father, Eric McGlover

For steadfastness: My grandmother, Gracie Goodin

For challenge: My aunt, Vanessa Franklin

For encouragement: My sister, Erin McGlover

For motivation: My son, Charles E. Bowens III

Thank you all for being examples of Christ's love.

res·to·ra·tion

/ˌrestəˈrāSH(ə)n/

noun

the action of returning something to a former owner, place, or condition.

Synonyms: repair, repairing, fixing, mending, refurbishment, reconditioning, rehabilitation, building, reconstruction, overhaul, redevelopment, renovation

val·ley

/ˈvalē/

noun

1. a low point or interval in any process, representation, or situation.

2. any place, period, or situation that is filled with fear, gloom, foreboding, or the like.

Synonyms: lowland, bottom, depression, hollow, hole, void, sink, sinkhole, pit

The valley can be a lonely and scary place, causing those who are suffering to experience feelings of confusion, shame, and abandonment, as if God does not care. But, the valley can also be a place of transformation and restoration—the place where people find new hope, increased strength, and gain a new perspective. This manual is designed to assist clergy and church leadership in becoming a guide during someone's valley experience, providing assurance that God has not forgotten about them.

WHAT SETS THIS MANUAL APART

- Resources can be utilized by all members of clergy and church leadership staff, as themes and diagnoses are commonly seen in all churches nationwide

- Offers background information for suicide prevention, schizophrenia spectrum and other psychotic disorders, clinical depression, bipolar disorder, domestic violence, substance abuse, homicide prevention, child sexual abuse, and child physical/emotional abuse and neglect

- Includes ethical and legal considerations, signs and symptoms related to each category, checklists and screening assessment tools, a list of national referral resources, and mental health agencies in Los Angeles County

- Facilitates greater awareness of the need to utilize churches in providing mental health resources to the communities they serve

- Extends psychological awareness through the use of links to national and local resources for common disorders clergy and lay ministry workers may encounter

- Acts as an intervention and consultation guide, giving non-clinically trained clergy tools to help eliminate confusion and to ease some feelings of anxiety when dealing with common mental health issues presented in the Church

- Offers a bridge between the Church community and mental health awareness and treatment, reaching marginalized populations and potentially reducing health disparities among groups

All forms and screening tools can be downloaded on our website under the Resources tab! Go to www.drvalindab.com and enter the code: RITVtools

LETTER FROM THE AUTHOR

> Where there is no counsel, the people fall.
> But in the multitude of counselors there is safety.
>
> PROVERBS 11:14 (KJV)

As a doctoral student, I was very interested in the state of mental health among African Americans and the reasons why we are hesitant to seek traditional mental health services. There is established research indicating a large health disparity between the utilization of traditional mental services and African-American help-seeking behavior. I also found that many socio-historical factors and barriers to treatment, including lack of trust, misdiagnosis, lack of access to care, poor quality of care, lack of knowledge, and social stigma, have greatly contributed to the African-American community's mistrust of the formal health care system. As a result, many African Americans turn to non-traditional community supports, such as the Black Church, clergy, and familial and social networks to meet their therapeutic needs. Given the trust between the Black Church and the community, and the stigma associated with utilizing traditional mental health services, many African Americans employ religious coping skills when dealing with psychological issues.

I grew up in the Black Church and am still a very active part of it today, so I know firsthand that the need for this information is great. Yet, there is still an underutilization of mental health resources in the religious community *at large*. It could be for those aforementioned reasons of socio-historical factors and barriers to treatment, but it could also be that many people of faith may believe that seeking mental health services equates to either an inability to handle issues independently, or a lack of faith in God's infinite power. In other words, seeking mental health services means one is demonstrating "spiritual weakness." This manual is designed to help dispel that belief and create awareness that **all** people, no matter how great their faith, will experience distress and overwhelming challenging situations at some point during their lives (Matthew 5:45). And, more importantly, that God places people in our lives to help us navigate through those uncertain circumstances (Galatians 6:2).

Given that all people experience distress and uncertainty at some point, and that *all* people can benefit from effective counsel, I realized that this information can be of assistance to not only clergy of the traditional Black Church, but to *all* clergy who need assistance in helping their congregants find resources for life's challenges.

Clergy play a vital role in their respective communities, as they take on the responsibility of counselors, advisors, and therapists to both congregants and community members. Thus, when congregants and members of the community have a psychological, emotional, and/or social issue, they may turn to the church looking for guidance. Financial problems? They go to the church. Children out of control? They turn to a minister. Marital issues? They turn to a minister for that, too. Educational, occupational, and housing resources? They turn

Letter from the Author

to the church. Emotional problems? Grief, loss, and bereavement? Legal issues? Psychological problems? Pastor, I need help! Oh yeah, and spiritual guidance? Clergy should, along with everything else, *definitely* have a handle on that, rightly dividing the word of truth, all while tending to and "fixing" the needs of their congregants. Given the great demand for clergy to meet the therapeutic needs of congregants, an increasing number of churches have been both training and utilizing lay counselors. The church is often (and has historically been) a one-stop shop where all needs should be met quickly and effectively. The good thing is that people trust the church with some of their most sensitive and private issues. The not-so-good thing is that often, clergy may receive little to no training in how to deal with the multitude of mental health issues presented by their congregants.

The inspiration for this manual came from my own personal experience at my church in South Los Angeles. My pastor, a beacon of light in his community, is called upon for everything! Sickness, finances, evangelism, children's ministry, everything! In addition to the host of problems he is expected to handle, I found that he was charged with counseling congregants as well. He has experienced everything from marital and family issues, to suicide, to congregants suffering from severe mental illness, grief and loss, depression, trauma, substance abuse, homelessness, domestic violence, child sexual abuse, and so much more.

I met with him one day after church and he said, "Sometimes I don't know what to do. I absolutely believe in the power of prayer. I also know that God gives us resources to help others, but I don't know where to turn." Right then I realized that for years I, too, thought that my pastor was superhuman, able to solve every problem. But in that intimate moment, in his honesty and vulnerability, I realized that the man of God needed help in order help the people! So, with a little (well, a lot) of research and with some insight from several licensed psychologists, pastoral counselors, ministers, and consultants, I put together this quick reference guide as my small contribution to help edify God's kingdom.

This manual is not an exhaustive resource for every problem encountered by clergy and church leadership staff. Rather, it focuses on common mental health issues of congregants encountered by clergy through their ministerial work, and highlights ways to identify symptoms, assess need for further treatment by a licensed mental health professional, and lists a host of resources for clergy to refer congregants to who are in need of further assistance. It's a sort of how-to guide. Further, this manual is not meant to transform clergy into clinical psychologists, nor is it created for those who are clinically trained. Instead, it acts as a guide that will point you in the right direction and help you to feel *empowered* when dealing with mental health issues in the church. I found during my dissertation research that many people often seek counsel from a member of clergy first, and with them they bring a host of issues (generally after they have become too crushing to handle alone). As one can imagine, knowing how to effectively intervene can be overwhelming and downright scary. And like my pastor and many of his counterparts, while they have the good intention to help those suffering from psychological issues, they may not know where to turn. Thus, this manual is intended to be an intervention and consultation guide, giving clergy tools to

Letter from the Author

feel equipped and empowered when counseling congregants, to help eliminate some of the confusion, and ease some feelings of anxiety when dealing with common mental health issues.

This manual will offer background information for common issues or disorders that may be encountered by clergy, including suicide prevention, schizophrenia spectrum and other psychotic disorders, clinical depression, bipolar disorder, domestic violence, substance abuse, homicide prevention, child sexual abuse, and child physical/emotional abuse and neglect. This manual will also include ethical and legal considerations, signs and symptoms related to each category, checklists and assessment tools, and a list of referral resources for clergy to offer congregants. All of the information included in this manual (outside of the resources in Appendix A, which are specifically for Los Angeles County) can be used by any clergy member nationwide. It is important to note that the information in this manual does not replace a professional mental health screening or diagnosis.

CONTENTS

What Sets This Manual Apart v
Letter from the Author vii
Acknowledgments..xv
A Note About Confidentiality xvii
Documentation..xxi
Administration Of Screening Tools And Checklists xxxv

PART ONE
Suicide Prevention... 1

PART TWO
Schizophrenia Spectrum & Other Psychotic Disorders................... 15
Clinical Depression... 25
Bipolar Disorder 33

PART THREE
Domestic Violence 43
Substance Abuse 57

PART FOUR
Homicide Prevention.. 69

PART FIVE
Child Abuse 77

Appendix A 95
Appendix B 131
Endnotes 135

ACKNOWLEDGMENTS

It took an entire village to help complete this project. Without the support of my many colleagues, friends, and family members, this vision would not have come to fruition.

First, I would like to thank my assistant, Stephanie Nieto, who wholeheartedly committed her time and effort to the completion of this project. For your diligence, your passion, your unending support, your work ethic, and your commitment to research for the betterment, advocacy, and well-being of others, I thank you. You are a Godsend. Without doubt, I could not have completed this project without you.

To my parents, Eric and Viola McGlover, thank you for always being there in support of my endeavors. Your love for me never goes unnoticed. This manual could not be accomplished without your commitment to my dreams. I thank God for blessing me with you both.

To my only son, Charles Eric Bowens III, who diligently and patiently waited for Mommy while I worked on this project. You are my biggest motivation indeed. I love you more than words can express.

To my good friend and legal counsel, Angelina Evans, Esq. Thank you for your advice and for taking time to ensure that the information presented in this manual is legally sound. I am grateful for your friendship and your expertise.

To Pastor Rodney J. Howard Sr., thank you for always seeking ways to help those who are in need. This manual was inspired because of you. I admire your commitment to God and the lives of others. Thank you for all that you do. Your insight is truly valued.

Reverend Gerald Bailey, I cannot thank you enough for your constant spiritual guidance and presence, not only while I completed this project, but in my life overall. Thank you for your prayers, passionate encouragement, spiritual perspective, and many hearty laughs. Your love for God and others is inspiring.

To the entire SEP Publishing Group, thank you for your commitment to this project. Your patience and diligence will never be forgotten.

Tsega Worku, LMFT, thank you for your gentle push throughout the duration of this project. Your encouragement means the world. You are appreciated.

To Dr. Erica Holmes, thank you for helping to develop the concept of this manual during my doctoral studies. Your mentorship and support are truly valued. I am grateful for you.

To those who read the manual and provided feedback, your thoughts and suggestions are invaluable. Thank you for offering your time.

There is no way this task could have been accomplished without the active support of my family and friends. Thank you all for your encouragement, patience, and prayers. Your actions of love kept me going. I love you all dearly, and you are sincerely appreciated.

A NOTE ABOUT CONFIDENTIALITY

Confidentiality refers to the ethical and legal responsibility of clergy not to disclose information shared with them by a congregant/advisee in a private setting. It is clergy's responsibility to safeguard congregants by not disclosing information without prior consent from the advisee. It is also important to understand the term **clergy-penitent privilege.** Clergy-penitent privilege is a recognized form of privileged communication that prevents clergy or counselors from disclosing confidential information disclosed between an advisor and advisee during a court proceeding.[1] While the privilege rules vary from state to state, each state has some form of privilege that protects the communication between clergy and advisee.

Although confidentiality is mandatory, and communication between clergy and congregant fall under clergy-penitent privilege, privilege is not absolute, as there are times that confidentially must be breached. The instances when confidentiality must be broken are called **limits to confidentiality.** Limits to confidentiality include:

- **Harm to self (suicidal intention)**
- **Harm to others (homicidal intention)**
- **Suspected or known child abuse**

It is also important to know that reporting requirements for each state vary, so seeking legal counsel to ensure your understanding of the law is strongly advised. If a congregant discloses this information to you, and after seeking professional legal consultation you determine that you are required to break confidentiality, you **must** take the proper steps to ensure the safety of your congregants and/or others. Don't worry: the proper steps are outlined in the appropriate section of this manual.

At the onset of the counseling relationship, it is imperative that you explain the limits to confidentiality. An example of this could be:

> "Everything that you say during our sessions will be confidential. However, there are times when I will have to break confidentiality in order to keep you and others safe. If you disclose information about child abuse, elder abuse, or the intention to harm yourself or others, I will have to call the proper authorities to ensure your safety and the safety of those involved. Do you have any questions?"

Be sure to use language that is appropriate for your audience. For example, when explaining the limits of confidentiality to children, you might say:

> "While we work together, everything that you share with me will stay between me and you; what you say will be safe. But, because my number one goal is to keep you safe, there are three times that you may share something with me and I will need to tell someone else who can help. The first is if you tell me that a grown-up is hurting you; the second is if you want to hurt someone else; and the third is if you want to hurt yourself. If you tell me any one of those three things, then I will have to call someone else so that we can keep you safe. Do you have any questions?"

A Note About Confidentiality

One more thing: Given that the counseling relationship between you and your congregant is confidential, by law you **cannot** give out any information about your counseling relationship. The exception to this rule is if you are served with a court subpoena, at which point you would refer to legal counsel.

Limits of confidentiality should be explained to both parents and minors. It is suggested that you outline the limits of confidentiality through written form by having your congregant sign an Informed Consent and Release of Liability Form (which will be explained in the Documentation section of this manual) and reiterate it verbally during your first meeting.

DOCUMENTATION

Documentation is crucial in tracking pertinent information when meeting with congregants/advisees. Appropriate documentation facilitates effective care in hopes that the congregant receives the appropriate professional assistance necessary while on their journey to healing. In this section, you will find pertinent information regarding informed consent, meeting notes, and referral forms. There are also three sample forms that you may adapt and use for your counseling ministry.

INFORMED CONSENT

Informed consent is a legal and ethical authorization given by a congregant/advisee to participate in mental health treatment, research, procedure, or clinical study. It is important that at the onset of a counseling relationship the guidelines, limits of confidentiality, and roles and responsibilities of the counselor/organization are clearly defined and the congregant/advisee has given consent for participation in counseling services. It is recommended that you give your congregant/advisee an Informed Consent and Release of Liability form *before* the first meeting so they have time to read the form in its entirety. It is also recommended that you go over each section of the form in detail during your first session to ensure congregant/client understanding and to answer any questions.

There are two sample consent forms included on the following pages that should be adapted, as appropriate, given your congregant/advisee population and organizational dynamics. The first form, Congregational Care Pastoral Counseling Disclosure and Informed Consent, can be best utilized for pastoral counseling. It outlines the nature of the pastoral counseling relationship, the background/qualifications of the pastor/minister, and limits of confidentiality. The second form, Informed Consent for Participation – Bible Guidance Ministry, can be best utilized for lay counseling or peer counseling ministries. It details the limits of counselor expertise and what can be expected from the counseling relationship, along with limits of confidentiality and supervision requirements. Legal consultation to ensure that the form includes proper state law is strongly suggested. **All forms and screening tools can be downloaded on our website under the Resources tab. Go to www.DrValindaB.com *and enter the code: RITVtools.***

CONGREGATIONAL CARE
PASTORAL COUNSELING DISCLOSURE AND INFORMED CONSENT

NATURE OF PASTORAL COUNSELING: As a ministry within Congregational Care, I am here to serve as a temporary support for you through pastoral counseling. In addition to our pastoral counseling relationship, I will also work with you to rally resources around you, both within our church community and with other health professionals, to help enrich your own growth.

MY CREDENTIALS: I have over 15 years of experience as a pastoral counselor, and over 20 years serving as an ordained minister. I graduated from the University of New Orleans with a Bachelor of Arts in Sociology; and from Dallas Theological Seminary with a Master's in Theology (ThM) majoring in Pastoral Leadership. I was ordained as a minister of the gospel of Jesus Christ in 1995. As part of my continuing education and professional development plan, I regularly pursue ongoing training and educational undertakings. My pastoral counseling is very strongly biblically based while integrating evidence-based theory, which is consistent with Scripture. The majority of my counseling work is with married couples that are seeking to develop their relationship into one that is more honoring to God and each other. However, I also work with those desiring pastoral support through grief, or guidance through other types of life's challenges, from a biblical perspective.

As a pastoral counselor, I am not required to attain a license issued by the state of Texas for the practice of professional counseling, marriage and family therapy, or social work specialties; nor am I pursuing the required education or training for such licenses.

MY APPROACH: As part of this professional disclosure, I would like to share with you my view on the nature of counseling and some basic information. My approach to counseling is anchored in biblically based theology that is congruent with the doctrinal statement of Hill Country Bible Church. You can find the doctrinal statement for HCBC at www.hcbc.com. I believe our intimate relationship with God is a vital part of the healing process for life's challenges we're facing today. Within that perspective, I will use prayer, application of biblical principles, and Scripture to help support and guide you through the challenges that may lead you to seek my guidance.

Our Pastoral Counseling Relationship:

Our Contact: Our relationship is strictly pastoral regarding your counseling, and I will work to relate to you respectfully and confidentially as your pastor at all times. Since I am a member of HCBC and a resident of the community surrounding our church, this may increase the likelihood of us running into one another around the church or even in the community, outside our planned appointments. If this occurs, I suggest we feel free to greet one another and be cordial, but I will commit to keeping the content of our appointments and anything related confidential. If you would like to discuss anything in regards to those sessions, please feel free to redirect that to our appointment times. If you would also like to introduce me to those who are around you, you are most welcome, but I will leave this step in your hands.

Confidentiality: The things shared within the counseling context are held in the strictest confidence and will in no way affect my pastoral care for you. I will work to provide a confidential place for you to share things that you may not feel safe sharing with others. While I work to hold your confidentiality with utmost regard, there are exceptions that will result in this privilege being waived, and those are listed as follows:

> **Reporting of child/elder/disabled abuse** – Upon hearing of child abuse, I am mandated by the state to disclose this to the proper authorities.
>
> **Threats to harm self or others** – I am mandated by law to disclose to the appropriate person, agency, or civil authorities any threats of harm that a person may attempt or desire to do to one's self or to others.

Consultation: Since I desire to give you support with excellence, I may seek consultation from other professionals on our staff to ensure that I am giving you the support you need. During consultation, your identifying information will be withheld so as to protect your confidentiality.

The Pastoral Counseling Process:

Discomfort: Sometimes when looking at painful events, past histories, or exploring options, it can bring up feelings of discomfort, and I invite you to share this with me. Oftentimes when working through these particular pieces, it can seem like things get a bit worse before they get a bit better. Please keep me updated with this process for you so I can be sure to get you the support you need.

Family/Couples support: For those who are seeking family or couples support, I will work to employ a "No Secrets" stance, in which I will not be gatekeeper to secrets that I believe will continue to perpetuate the challenges in your marriage/family. Individual appointments within a family/marital context are used to assist the individual towards the larger family/marital goal. I may choose to not disclose private content from individual sessions by using my own discretion and judgment in regards to your goals. An exception to this would be if you tell me that you or another family member is at risk, in which case I will act to protect that person as the primary goal.

Temporary support: My role as a pastoral counselor is designed to walk alongside people in order to meet the need of the moment. Although it is challenging to quantify how much time the pastoral counseling process will take for each person, our resources currently limit our ability to maintain long-term counseling. Therefore, our appointments will be more short-term in nature, not to exceed 12 to 18 sessions. If longer care is needed, I will provide you with adequate referrals and resources to help you continue in your growth.

Resolution of disagreements: If there is any disagreement or tension that should arise between the person receiving ministry and myself regarding the counseling session, please first bring this to your appointments with me. I want to be able to work through issues with you as they may arise. If the dispute cannot be resolved at this level, all parties will then agree and request support from the church's executive senior staff team for full and final resolution.

Waiver of liability: In consideration for receiving any form of counseling from the Pastoral Counseling Ministry of HCBC, the person receiving the counseling agrees to release and waive any and all claims of any kind against the ministry, staff, interns, lay counselor(s), or the church that may arise from, result from, or be related to conduct or advice given.

No court testimony: The counseling we provide is faith-based and spiritual in nature. Texas law prohibits compelled disclosure of these counseling exchanges, notes, or records in any court of law. Accordingly, our counseling team will not provide court testimony, and by signing below you are acknowledging this strict confidentiality and further agree that neither you nor your legal representative will attempt to subpoena your counselor for testimony.

Your Commitment:

Commitment to participate: Your role in our pastoral relationship is to commit to the process and participate to the best of your ability. Please plan to be consistently present and to put in your best effort to help contribute to the process.

Commitment to complete homework: Your commitment continues outside of sessions, as we may decide that homework would facilitate your progress.

Commitment of notice of termination: Either one of us may choose to end our counseling at any time, but my preference would be for us to give one another a week's notice in order to transition you, as well as end our time well.

Commitment to maintain and schedule appointments: This commitment includes holding and keeping our appointment times consistently and with timeliness. Since this is a small resource for our large community, I would ask that we mutually respect the time that we have scheduled for our appointments. If you need to reschedule, please do so through the congregational care administrator 48 hours in advance. You may contact him/her at xxx-xxx-xxx to schedule and maintain your appointments with me. If you are unable/unwilling to be on time and consistent in upholding your appointment time, it may result in your future appointments being cancelled in order to make room for others seeking my services.

EMERGENCIES: If you are in an emergency, please contact your local hospital or local police department by dialing 9-1-1 when necessary and appropriate. If it is after hours and you would like to talk to someone from Hill Country, you can call the Minister On Call at xxx-xxx-xxxx and follow the prompts to connect with the MOC. Please update me at your next session about any medical or mental health emergencies that do occur.

Documentation

I have carefully read, understand, and agree to comply with the information above.

_____
Congregant/Advisee Name (Print)   Signature   Date

_____
Congregant/Advisee Name (Print)   Signature   Date

*Hill Country Bible Church's Congregational Care Pastoral Counseling Disclosure and Informed Consent form, used with permission.

Restoration in the Valley: A Psychological Resource Manual for Clergy

INFORMED CONSENT FOR PARTICIPATION

Biblical Guidance Ministry

The Biblical Guidance Ministry (BGM) team consists of non-staff volunteers of Hill Country Bible Church who have a deep passion to walk with people from all phases of life by offering biblical support and encouragement. Each team member is under the direction of Pastor _____ and has completed training in the context of biblical guidance.

While the team members of the Biblical Counseling Ministry are not professional counselors, do not hold a counseling license, and are not trained as professional counselors, they have been specifically screened and trained to utilize Scripture to help inspire healing through the life-changing reality of Jesus Christ. Due to this being more of a peer ministry, there will be no formal documentation or files that contain information about your conversations. Diagnosing, psychological evaluations, legal guidance, and involvement in your legal proceedings are therefore not a part of this ministry.

Participants will be matched with a team member of the same gender and will meet at a predetermined time and in a public place that provides an appropriate level of confidentiality. The number of meetings you have will be determined by the progress or benefit that both you and the BGM team member can freely discuss at any point in time. The BGM team member may also refer you to other ministries in our church or to alternate resources to help support you in your journey.

We value the time that our team members are spending with you. Therefore, each member of our team is actively involved in his or her own supervision. In supervision, information about the content of your conversations may be shared, but out of respect for you, names and identifying information will be exempt from those conversations.

Since this ministry has a high regard for your safety, your Biblical Guidance Ministry team member will disclose to their supervisor the following types of information:

- **information regarding abuse or neglect of a child, disabled, or elderly person**
- **information regarding self-harm or intent to take harmful action against another**
- **information about ongoing behavior that could be potentially**
- **damaging to others or a church ministry**

If your Biblical Guidance Team member becomes concerned about any of these items, your safety, or the safety of others, they may disclose the name and parties involved to their direct supervisor to ensure proper care is administered to each party.

By signing below you are consenting to participate in the Biblical Guidance Ministry, understanding the role and qualifications of the team member who is serving you.

Signature of Participant or Legal Guardian   Date

Signature of Participant or Legal Guardian   Date

*Hill Country Bible Church's Congregational Informed Consent for Participation - Biblical Guidance Ministry form, adapted with permission.

MEETING NOTES

In writing this manual, I wanted to make sure that the information I provided protected the interest of clergy, lay counseling members, and congregants. After much research and legal consultation, I decided against including information about how to take meeting notes and store the confidential information of advisees, as it may result in legal consequences for spiritual advisors. For example, notes that contain confidential information may be confiscated or subpoenaed, potentially placing the clergy at risk for unauthorized breach of confidentiality and risking undue congregant/advisee harm. What I will say is that when reportable events occur (i.e., child or elder abuse, harm to self, or harm to others), refraining from taking notes should never be used as a vehicle for clergy to circumvent the mandatory reporting laws. Inform the proper authorities and make the necessary reports so that you do not risk further legal or ethical harm. Required steps are outlined in each section of this manual. As usual, legal consultation is strongly advised.

REFERRAL FORM

The Referral Form is the form that you will complete and give to the congregant with information regarding professional mental health services or other resource recommendations. It is intended to assist the congregant in following up on the referrals that you recommended during your meeting. Before giving the congregant the completed form, be sure to write down the names of the referral sources at the bottom of your meeting notes. Remember that while you may hope and/or insist that a congregant seek professional treatment, they are not required to do so.

REFERRAL FORM

Referral 1

Name/Organization:_____

Date: _____

Address: _____

E-mail/Website: _____

Phone number: _____

Referral 2

Name/Organization:_____

Date: _____

Address: _____

E-mail/Website: _____

Phone number: _____

Referral 3

Name/Organization:_____

Date: _____

Address: _____

E-mail/Website: _____

Phone number: _____

ADMINISTRATION OF SCREENING TOOLS AND CHECKLISTS

In each section of the manual, you will find a screening tool or checklist with symptoms or criteria related to certain clinical diagnoses. You can give the screen to the congregant/advisee to complete or you may ask them the questions and record their responses. Given that these tools are provided to assist the congregant in seeking help from a mental health professional, here are a few important guidelines to remember:

DO

- Give the congregant a copy of the screening tool/checklist to complete in your office or at home
- Encourage them to take the completed tool to the doctor or mental health professional
- Remind them that treatment is important
- Follow up with congregant
- Send a message of hope, care, and concern

DO NOT

- Keep a copy of a congregant's completed screening tool/checklist

- Attempt to diagnose the congregant. Remember, only a professionally trained mental health therapist can diagnose
- Share results of the screening tool/checklist with others unless necessary. For example, if someone completed a checklist and is actively suicidal, then you would call the appropriate authorities. More detailed information is available in the Suicide section of this manual

All forms and screening tools can be downloaded on our website under the Resources tab. Go to www.DrValindaB.com and enter the code: RITVtools

PART ONE

✓ SUICIDE PREVENTION

All forms and screening tools can be downloaded on our website under the Resources tab. Go to www.DrValindaB.com and enter the code: RITVtools

DISCLAIMER: THESE CHECKLISTS ARE NOT INTENDED FOR DIAGNOSTIC OR TREATMENT PURPOSES. THEY ARE NOT A SUBSTITUTE FOR ASSESSMENT OR ADVICE FROM A LICENSED PROFESSIONAL.

SUICIDE PREVENTION

Suicide is a devastating tragedy that impacts people of all ages, racial and ethnic background, socioeconomic status, religion, and educational level. It often occurs when life stressors exceed current coping abilities. According to the American Foundation for Suicide Prevention[2], suicide was the tenth leading cause of death in the United States in 2015. In 2015 alone, 44,193 Americans committed suicide. That's approximately 121 suicides per day. In that same year, 494,169 people sought medical attention for self-inflicted injuries. Death by firearms accounts for 50 percent of all suicides.

Consistent with the statistics for the nation, suicide is the tenth leading cause of death in the state of California as well, according to the California Department of Mental Health, Office of Suicide Prevention.[3] Approximately 3,300 Californians commit suicide annually. Nine Californians die by means of suicide per day, and death by suicide is more frequently reported in California than homicide.[4]

Given these alarming statistics, as well as the psychological implications of the victims and their families and the stigma that can be associated with suicide, it is important for clergy to be able to identify risk factors, protective factors, and warning signs. Learning to conduct an accurate suicide assessment and employ appropriate intervention strategies to help prevent suicide and ensure safety can save someone's life! **Suicide is preventable.**

Suicide Risk Factors

Risk factors, different from warning signs, are the elements that increase the likelihood that individuals will consider, attempt, or encounter death by suicide.[5] Some risk factors include:

- Prior history of suicidal behavior, including suicidal attempts and/or self-injurious behavior
- Previous or current psychiatric disorders such as mood disorders, substance abuse, Attention Deficit Hyperactivity Disorder (ADHD), Traumatic Brain Injury, Post-Traumatic Stress Disorder (PTSD), Antisocial, Histrionic, Narcissistic, Borderline Personality Disorders, and recent onset of illness
- Family history of suicidal behavior
- Stressors such as family turmoil or triggering events that lead to shame, humiliation, or extreme sadness, loss, or long-term medical illness
- History of physical and/or sexual abuse
- Social isolation
- Barriers to mental health treatment
- Cultural and religious beliefs that suicide is a noble act
- Access to firearms
- Individuals in the veteran, homeless, immigrant, and LGBTQ population

Suicide Protective Factors

Protective factors are characteristics that decrease the likelihood that individuals will consider, attempt, or encounter death by suicide.[6]

Some protective factors include:

- Connection to family, social networks, community, and social institutions
- Ability to cope with stress and solve problems effectively
- Cultural and religious beliefs that offer hope and discourage suicide
- Sense of responsibility to family
- Effective and supportive medical and mental health care relationships

Suicide Warning Signs

"Take any suicidal talk or behavior seriously. It's not just a warning sign that the person is thinking about suicide—it's a cry for help."[7]

Warning signs are "the behavioral manifestations of precipitating conditions in a particular individual. They are directly observable, reflect the current state of the individual, and indicate the presence of a suicidal crisis."[8] Suicide warning signs include, but are not limited to:

- Threatening to hurt or kill oneself
- Devising a plan to acquire means to kill themselves (i.e., purchasing a gun)
- Talking or writing about death, dying, or suicide
- Feelings of hopelessness
- Feelings of being a burden to others
- Giving away personal possessions
- Withdrawal/social isolation
- Extreme mood swings
- Showing rage or talking about seeking revenge
- Increased use of alcohol and drugs
- Increased levels of anxiety or agitation
- Reckless behavior
- Finalizing personal affairs (i.e., creating a will)
- Increased or decreased need for sleep

If you have reason to believe that one of your congregants is suicidal, do not sit passively! Ask direct questions! Use the *ABC Suicide Assessment* on the following page to help you start the conversation. *For youth, inform parent/guardian in addition to mental health and law enforcement professionals.

ABC SUICIDE ASSESSMENT

Name: _____ **Date:** _____

Instructions to congregant: Please answer each question to the best of your ability

Instructions to minister: Ask each question to congregant. Ask for more detail as needed.

A. Risk Assessment	1.	Do you have any history of suicidal behavior, including suicidal attempts and/or self-injurious behavior?
	2.	Do you have any previous or current psychiatric disorders?
	3.	Is there family history of suicidal behavior?
	4.	Have you experienced stressors that make you feel that your life is not worth living?
	5.	Do you have any history of physical and/or sexual abuse?
	6.	Do you have access to firearms?
B. Protective Factors	1.	Do you have someone to talk about your problems with?
	2.	Do you have people who are relying on you (i.e., children or family members?
	3.	Do you have someone who is sharing your experience?
	4.	How do you deal with stress?

C. Suicide details	1. How often do you have thoughts about killing yourself?
	2. How long do these thoughts last?
	3. When was the last time you had these thoughts?
	4. What has happened that makes this life not worth living?
	5. What, if any, are reasons that keep you from fulfilling these thoughts?
	6. Tell me more about your plans for suicide (intended day, location, method).

•••

THIS INSTRUMENT IS DESIGNED FOR SCREENING PURPOSES
ONLY AND IS NOT TO BE USED AS A DIAGNOSTIC TOOL.

•••

SUICIDE ASSESSMENT AND REFERRAL SUGGESTIONS

Assessment Response	Ministerial Suggested Actions
Low Risk	
Responds "Yes" to 0-1 question(s) in risk assessment section.	No direct referral needed at this time.
Responds "Yes" to 2-3 questions in protective factors section.	Monitor as needed.
Gives a positive stress management response for question B-4.	Encourage social support through family, friends, and community resources.
Gives little to no positive response to having suicidal ideation.	Provide message of care, support, guidance, and prayer.
Moderate Risk	
Responds "Yes" to 2-4 questions in risk assessment section.	Give referral resources and suggest professional help.
Responds "Yes" to 1-2 questions in protective factors section.	Keep in contact with congregant.
Gives a positive and a negative stress management response for question B-4.	Encourage social support through family, friends, and community resources.
Gives unclear positive response to suicidal ideations.	Provide message of care, support, guidance, and prayer.
Gives some response to self-harm-related actions	

Assessment Response	Ministerial Suggested Actions
High Risk	
Responds "Yes" to 4-6 questions in risk assessment section. Responds "Yes" to 0-1 question in protective factors section. Gives a primarily negative stress management response for question B-4. Gives clear positive response to suicidal ideations with frequent suicidal thoughts that are intense and enduring. Has clear/specific plan on suicide	Call Psychiatric Mobile Response Team (PMRT) 1-800-854-7771 (LA County). Call 9-1-1 if PMRT is not available. Keep in contact with congregant. Encourage social support through family, friends, and community resources. Provide message of care, support, guidance, and prayer.

End of Section Checklist

- ☐ Complete the assessment
- ☐ Contact the proper authorities
- ☐ If minor, contact parents
- ☐ Give congregant resources/referrals
- ☐ Offer a message of hope, care, and concern

"God is bigger than your fears, stronger than your pain, and wiser than your thoughts. Trust Him! He's got this!"

1 CORINTHIANS 1:25

Part One / Suicide Prevention

SUICIDE PREVENTION RESOURCES

(Includes Los Angeles County Resources) *as of August 2016*

Los Angeles County Human Services Hotline:
Dial "2-1-1" (24 hours | Bilingual)
https://www.211la.org

For LA County Mental Health Agencies, please see
"Los Angeles County Resources" in Appendix A

Psychiatric Mobile Response Team, L.A. County
800-854-7771
Hearing Impaired: 562-651-2549

NATIONAL RESOURCES

National Suicide Prevention Lifeline
www.suicidepreventionlifeline.org
800-273-8255 (24-hour hotline)

Action Alliance for Suicide Prevention
www.actionallianceforsuicideprevention.org
202-572-3737

American Foundation for Suicide Prevention
www.afsp.org
Toll-Free: 1-888-333-AFSP (2377)

Center for Disease Control
www.cdc.gov/violenceprevention/suicide/
800-232-4636

National Institute of Mental Health
https://www.nimh.nih.gov/health/topics/suicide-prevention/index.shtml
866-615-6464

LOS ANGELES COUNTY RESOURCES

Los Angeles County Department of Mental Health
800-854-7771

California Youth Crisis Line
800-843-5200

Didi Hirsch Suicide Prevention Hotline
877-727-4747

LAPD Mental Health Evaluation Unit
213-996-1300

Los Angeles County Sheriff Mental Health
800-854-7771

Los Angeles County Youth Suicide Prevention Project
http://preventsuicide.lacoe.edu/

Suicide Prevention Center Hotline
877-7-CRISIS or
877-727-4747
Toll Free in L.A. and Orange Counties

Teen Line
800-TLC-TEEN
800-852-8336

Toll free in CA only. 6pm – 10pm PST
Trevor Lifeline-LGBTQ
866-488-7386

SELECTED READING MATERIALS

Biebel, D., & Foster, S. (2011). *Finding Your Way After the Suicide of Someone You Love*.

Black, J. (2003). *Suicide: Understanding and Intervening*.

Franklin, C., & Fong, R. (2011). *The Church Leader's Counseling Resource Book: A Guide to Mental Health and Social Problems*.

Hunt, J. (2013). *Suicide Prevention: Hope When Life Seems Hopeless*.

Kolf, J. (2002). *Standing in the Shadow: Help and Encouragement for Suicide Survivors*.

Mason, K. (2014). *Preventing Suicide: A Handbook for Pastors, Chaplains, and Pastoral Counselors*.

Swetland, K. (2005). *Facing Messy Stuff in the Church: Case Studies for Pastors and Congregations*.

Taylor, L. (2015). *As Many As I Love - Suicide, the Church, and the Believer*.

Townsend, L. (2006). *Suicide: Pastoral Responses*.

PART TWO

- ✓ SCHIZOPHRENIA SPECTRUM & OTHER PSYCHOTIC DISORDERS
- ✓ CLINICAL DEPRESSION
- ✓ BIPOLAR DIORDER

All forms and screening tools can be downloaded on our website under the Resources tab. Go to www.DrValindaB.com and enter the code: RITVtools

DISCLAIMER: THESE CHECKLISTS ARE NOT INTENDED FOR DIAGNOSTIC OR TREATMENT PURPOSES. THEY ARE NOT A SUBSTITUTE FOR ASSESSMENT OR ADVICE FROM A LICENSED PROFESSIONAL.

SCHIZOPHRENIA SPECTRUM & OTHER PSYCHOTIC DISORDERS

The *Diagnostic and Statistical Manual of Mental Disorders, Fifth Edition*, published by the American Psychiatric Association,[9] is the standard method of classifying mental health disorders among mental health professionals in the United States. According to the *DSM-5*, a mental disorder is defined as:

A syndrome characterized by clinically significant disturbance in an individual's cognition, emotion regulation, or behavior that reflects a dysfunction in the psychological, biological, or developmental processes underlying mental functioning. Mental disorders are usually associated with significant distress or disability in social, occupational, or other important activities. An acceptable or culturally approved response to a common stressor or loss, such as the death of a loved one, is not a mental disorder. Socially deviant behavior (e.g., political, religious, or sexual) and conflict primarily between the individual and society are not mental disorders unless deviance or conflicts results from a dysfunction in the individual, as described above. (p. 20).[10]

To simplify, Comer[11] referred to patterns of psychological abnormality as the Four D's.

Four D's of Psychological Abnormality

Different. Different, extreme, unusual, perhaps even bizarre

Distressing. Unpleasant and unsettling to the individual

Dysfunctional. Interfering with the person's ability to conduct daily activities in a constructive way

Dangerous. Interfering with the person's ability to conduct daily activities in a constructive way

While the disorders listed in the *DSM-5* vary in intensity and duration, this section of the manual will refer to disorders that are extreme in severity. The following signs or symptoms will help to assess for increased impairment. Please note that not all of the symptoms have to be present, and that each symptom may vary in severity. Look at the following table to identify presence and severity of each symptom as experienced by congregant or through subjective report or observation during the past seven days. While clergy are not clinically trained in the use of the *DSM-5* and are therefore unable to diagnose, this information is to simply offer some clarity into what your congregant may be experiencing. The terms **hallucination, delusion, disorganized thinking, grossly disorganized/abnormal motor behavior,** and **negative symptoms** are defined by the American Psychiatric Association.[12]

Hallucination

Occurs when a person perceives something that does not really exist. A hallucination can occur in one or all five senses.

👁	Seeing things that are not there or that other people cannot see.
👂	Hearing voices that other people cannot hear.
✋	Feeling things that other people don't feel, or feeling something touching your skin that isn't there.
👃	Smelling things that other people cannot smell, or not smelling the same thing that other people do smell.
🦷	Unpleasant taste in the mouth although nothing unpleasant has been eaten.

Delusion

A strong belief that is maintained even though there is great opposing evidence. Types of delusions include:

Persecutory. Delusions that an individual (or a person to whom the individual is close) is being maliciously mistreated.

Somatic. False belief about one's body such as a physical defect or medical condition. For example, the thought that something foreign is inside of, or passing through the body.

Jealous. Delusions that the individual's sexual partner is unfaithful.

Grandiose. Delusions of inflated worth, knowledge, power, identity, or special relationship to a deity or famous person

Erotomanic. An individual's false belief that another person, usually of higher status, is in love with him or her.

Mixed. Delusions characteristic of more than one of the above types but no one theme predominates

Disorganized Thinking

Occurs when people have disturbed, disrupted, and confused thought patterns that are usually inferred from an individual's speech. These changes in speech include:

	Rapid and constant speech.
	Giving answers that are completely unrelated to the questions that are being asked.
	Random speech or "word salad."
	Sudden loss in train of thought, causing an abrupt silence.

Grossly Disorganized/Abnormal Motor Behavior

An abnormal condition characterized by loss of bodily control. These actions may be characterized by:

	Dazed or inactive.
	Mania; hyperactivity or being "all over the place," especially at inappropriate times.
	Extreme rigidity or extreme flexibility of the limbs.

Part Two / Schizophrenia Spectrum & Other Psychotic Disorders

PSYCHOSIS DISORDER ASSESSMENT

Name: _____ Date: _____

Instructions: Please answer each question to the best of your ability.

	Y/N
I can see/hear things that others say they cannot see or hear.	
I've heard vivid conversations of two or more people in my head that others say are not present.	
I feel that my thoughts are not safe inside my head because someone is listening to me.	
I believe that I have superpowers.	
The voices inside my head are preventing me from doing normal activities.	
I sometimes have unexpected flexibility/rigidity in my limbs.	
I think I can see the future/distant past.	
I have had times when I have difficulty expressing myself with words or have been told that what I am saying does not make any sense.	
Sometimes my thoughts race so fast I don't have time to think things through.	
I sometimes feel there is someone who actively tells me what to do inside my head.	
My relationships suffer because of the voices I hear.	
There is a history of hearing voices/seeing people in my family.	

THIS INSTRUMENT IS DESIGNED FOR SCREENING PURPOSES ONLY AND IS NOT TO BE USED AS A DIAGNOSTIC TOOL.

End of Section Checklist

- ☐ Complete the assessment
- ☐ Give congregant resources/referrals
- ☐ Offer a message of hope, care, and concern

"Through the good and bad, ups and downs,
God hasn't changed His mind about you!

NUMBERS 23:19

SCHIZOPHRENIA SPECTRUM & OTHER PSYCHOTIC DISORDER RESOURCES

*Los Angeles County Human Services Hotline:
Dial "2-1-1" (24 hours | Bilingual)
https://www.211la.org*

*For LA County Mental Health Agencies, please see
"Los Angeles County Resources" in Appendix A*

NATIONAL RESOURCES

Schizophrenia and Related Disorders Alliance of America (SARDAA)
www.sardaa.org
800-493-2094

National Alliance on Mental Illness
1-800-950-6264
http://www.nami.org/Learn-More/Mental-Health-Conditions/Schizophrenia

National Schizophrenia Foundation
www.NSFoundation.org

Open the Doors
www.openthedoors.com

Schizophrenia and Related Disorders Alliance of America (SARDAA)
www.sardaa.org
800-493-2094

Schizophrenia.com
www.schizophrenia.com

The Menninger Clinic
www.menningerclinic.com

World Fellowship for Schizophrenia & Allied Disorders
www.world-schizophrenia.org
416-961-2855

SELECTED READING MATERIALS

Amador, X. (2007). *I Am Not Sick I Don't Need Help: How to Help Someone with Mental Illness Accept Treatment.*

Brown, L. (2016). *Schizophrenia: The Complete Beginners Guide To Understanding Schizophrenia Symptoms, Diagnosis And Treatment!*

De Hert, M. (2003). *The Secret of the Brain Chip: A Self-Help Guide for People Experiencing Psychosis.*

LaFond, V. (2002). *Grieving Mental Illness: A Guide for Patients and Their Caregivers.*

Mueser, K., & Gingerich, S. (2006). *The Complete Family Guide to Schizophrenia - Helping Your Loved One Get the Most Out of Life.*

Peters, S. (2015). *Schizophrenia: The Ultimate Guide To Schizophrenia - Learn The Causes, Symptoms, Types, And Early Warning Signs Of Schizophrenia!*

Rice, A. (2015). *Schizophrenia: You're Not Insane: Understanding Schizophrenia, Misdiagnosis, Current Research, Recovery, And The Violent Few.*

Rivers, C. (2014). *Schizophrenia: Enter the Mind of a Schizophrenic! The Ultimate Information Book.*

Ross, M. (2008). *Schizophrenia: Medicine's Mystery, Society's Shame.*

Schizophrenia Society of Canada. (2000). *Learning About Schizophrenia: Rays of Hope: A Reference Manual for Families and Caregivers.*

Schiller, L. (1996). *The Quiet Room: A Journey Out of the Torment of Madness.*

Simpson, Amy. (2013). *Troubled Minds: Mental Illness and the Church's Mission.*

Snyder, K. (2007). *Me, Myself, and Them: A Firsthand Account of One Young Person's Experience with Schizophrenia. Adolescent Mental Health Initiative.*

Torrey, E. (2013). *Surviving Schizophrenia: A Manual for Families, Consumers and Providers.*

Wasow, M. (2000). *The Skipping Stone: Ripple Effects of Mental Illness on the Family.*

CLINICAL DEPRESSION

There are times when everyone feels sad, hopeless, or lonely. However, major depression (referred to as clinical depression) often lasts for a longer period of time and is debilitating. Clergy often encounter congregants who are dealing with loss, grief, and bereavement. While each individual may react differently to grief and loss, it is imperative that clergy are able to assess the difference between sadness and clinical depression so that congregants can be referred to appropriate treatment resources. Moreover, although a congregant may say that they are "depressed," it is important to understand the true definition of clinical depression and when to refer a congregant to the appropriate resources to receive additional assistance by clinically trained personnel.

While there are several types of depression differing in presentation, onset (when it started), frequency, and intensity, the one discussed in this crisis intervention manual is Major Depressive Disorder. Five or more of these symptoms have to be present during the same 2-week period.[13]

Major Depressive Disorder Symptoms

1. An individual has experienced five (or more) of the following symptoms during the same 2-week period. These symptoms represent a change from previous functioning. At least one of the following

symptoms is either depressed mood, or loss of interest or pleasure in life/activities. Be sure to exclude symptoms that are clearly caused by another medical condition.

- Depressed mood or loss of interest/pleasure most of the day, almost every day (may look like irritable behavior in children and adolescents)
- Loss of energy
- Feeling hopeless and worthless or excessively guilty
- Sleeping either too much or too little
- Loss of interest and enjoyment in activities
- Weight loss or weight gain
- Difficulty concentrating or making decisions
- Frequent thoughts about death or suicide, or suicide attempts
- Feeling tired

2. The symptoms cause significant distress or impairment in social, occupational, or other important areas of functioning.

3. The depression is not due to the physiological effects of a substance or another medical condition.

As you are sitting with your congregant, you can administer the Patient Health Questionnaire (PHQ-9).[14] The PHQ-9 is a validated screening tool used to assess clinical depression. Once the congregant completes the screen, please be sure to encourage them to seek professional mental health services and take the completed screen with them to one of the referral resources that you recommend. For specific locations in Los Angeles County, please see Appendix A.

THE PATIENT HEALTH QUESTIONNAIRE (PHQ-9)

	Not at all (0 pts)	Several days (1 pts)	More than half the days (2 pts)	Nearly every day (3 pts)
Little interest or pleasure in doing things				
Feeling down, depressed, or hopeless				
Trouble falling/staying asleep or sleeping too much				
Feeling tired or having little energy				
Poor appetite or overeating				
Feeling bad about yourself/think that you are a failure/think that you have let yourself or loved ones down				
Trouble concentrating on things such as reading the newspaper or watching television				
Moving or speaking so slowly that other people have noticed. Or the opposite—being so fidgety or restless that you have been moving around a lot more than usual				
Have thoughts that you would be better off dead, or of hurting yourself in some way				
Add total (0-27 points total)				

Name: _____ Date: _____

Instructions: Over the last two weeks, how often have you been bothered by any of the following problems?

	To what degree did the above questions make it difficult for you to do your work/take care of things at home/get along with other people? (Check the selection that applies.)
No Difficulty	
Somewhat Difficult	
Very Difficult	
Extremely Difficult	

Score	Symptom Level
0–4	No Depression
5–9	Minimal depression
10–14	Mild depression**
15–19	Moderate depression**
20–27	Severe depression **

Congregant is **at risk for suicide. Please complete the suicide screener in the Suicide Prevention section of this manual, refer congregant to appropriate resources, and if necessary, contact the appropriate emergency psychiatric response team or call 9-1-1.

Developed by Kroenke, Spitzer, and Williams (1994). No permission required to reproduce, translate, display or distribute.

Part Two / Clinical Depression

·······································
THIS INSTRUMENT IS DESIGNED FOR SCREENING PURPOSES ONLY AND IS NOT TO BE USED AS A DIAGNOSTIC TOOL.
·······································

End of Section Checklist

- ☐ Complete the assessment
- ☐ If determined that congregant is at risk for suicide, complete suicide screener found in the suicide section of this manual and contact the appropriate emergency psychiatric response team or call 9-1-1
- ☐ Give congregant resources/referrals
- ☐ Offer a message of hope, care, and concern

"When we fill our thoughts with the right things, the wrong ones have no room to enter"

JOYCE MEYER

CLINICAL DEPRESSION RESOURCES

Los Angeles County Human Services Hotline:
Dial "2-1-1" (24 hours | Bilingual)
https://www.211la.org

For LA County Mental Health Agencies, please see
"Los Angeles County Resources" in Appendix A

NATIONAL RESOURCES

Anxiety and Depression Association of America
www.adaa.org
240-485-1001

American Academy of Child &
Adolescent Psychiatry
https://www.aacap.org/AACAP/Families_and_Youth/Facts_for_Families/FFF-Guide/The-Depressed-Child-004.aspx

American Psychological Association Help Center
http://www.apa.org/helpcenter/depression.aspx
800-374-2721

Depression and Bipolar Support Alliance
www.dbsalliance.org
800-826-3632

Depression.org
800-239-1265
www.depression.org

Freedom from Fear: Anxiety and Depression Resource Organization
www.freedomfromfear.org
718-351-1717 x20

Families for Depression Awareness
www.familyaware.org
800-273-TALK

Mental Health America
http://www.mentalhealthamerica.net/conditions/depression
800-969-6642

National Alliance on Mental Illness
http://www.nami.org/Learn-More/Mental-Health-Conditions/Depression
800-950-6264

National Institute of Mental Health
https://www.nimh.nih.gov/health/topics/depression/index.shtml
866-615-6464

Suicide Awareness Voices of Education
www.save.org
952-946-7998

We Search Together
www.wesearchtogether.org
866-487-0510

SELECTED READING MATERIALS

Hall, A. (2014). *Depression in the Church: Is it Spiritual, or Is It Physical?*

Hermes, K. (2011). *Prayers for Surviving Depression.*

Janaro, J. (2010). *Never Give Up: My Life and God's Mercy.*

Knier, R. (2013). *New Wine: Mental Illness and the Church.*

Kraniak, S. (2015). *Depression, Anxiety, and The Child of God.*

Meyer, J. (2000). Me, Myself, and I. How to Be Delivered from Yourself. [CD]. Fenton, MO: Joyce Meyer Ministries.

Morris, S. (2011). *40 Days to Better Living—Depression.*

Simpson, A. (2013). *Troubled Minds: Mental Illness and the Church's Mission.*

Starghill, B. (2012). *Mocked, Vilified, and Caricatured. A Theological Response for Clinically Depressed African-American Men.*

Tan, S., & Ortberg, J. (2004). *Coping with Depression.*

Vandagriff, D. (2011). *Deliverance from Depression: Finding Hope and Healing Through the Atonement of Christ.*

Welch, E. (2000). *Depression: The Way Up When You Are Down.*

BIPOLAR DISORDER

Bipolar disorder is a chronic mental illness that causes drastic shifts in mood, energy, and the ability to think clearly and carry out daily tasks. According to the National Alliance on Mental Health,[15] Bipolar Disorder is diagnosed in 2.9 percent of the US population, with 83 percent of the cases being classified as severe. Bipolar Disorder affects men and women equally, and while the disorder can be seen at any age, the average age of onset is 25.

Individuals with Bipolar Disorder experience shifts in mood from high to low that are more extreme than the mood swings that are experienced by people without the disorder. If left untreated, symptoms tend to get worse. It is important to note that the lifetime risk of suicide for individuals with Bipolar Disorder is approximately 15 times that of the general population.[16]

Moods generally range from periods of mania (or manic episodes) to very depressed states (or depressive episodes). **Mania** can be described as excessively cheerful, euphoric, high, or energized behavior, while **depressive states** are very sad, hopeless states. Less severe manic episodes are known as **hypomanic episodes**. There are four basic types of Bipolar Disorder, but for the purposes of this manual, three are discussed below:

Bipolar I Disorder—characterized by manic episodes that last at least one week and are present most of the day, or by manic symptoms that are so severe that the person needs immediate hospital care. Usually, depressive episodes (which can be either depressed mood or loss of interest/pleasure) occur as well, typically lasting at least two weeks. Experiencing depression and manic symptoms at the same time (known as depression with mixed features) is also possible.

Bipolar II Disorder—characterized by a pattern of depressive episodes and hypomanic episodes.

Cyclothymic Disorder—defined by numerous periods of hypomanic symptoms as well as numerous periods of depressive symptoms lasting for at least two years (one year in children and adolescents). Simply put, Cyclothymic Disorder is a constant state of depression/depressive symptoms for at least two years. However, the symptoms do not meet the diagnostic criteria for a hypomanic episode and a depressive episode.

Signs & Symptoms

The following symptoms represent a significant and noticeable change from usual behavior:

Manic Symptoms	Depressive Symptoms
<ul><li>Easily distracted</li><li>Decreased need for sleep</li><li>Talking very rapidly or talking excessively</li><li>Feeling agitated or irritable</li></ul>	<ul><li>Depressed mood most of the day, almost every day (may look like irritable behavior in children and adolescents)</li><li>Loss of energy</li></ul>

Manic Symptoms	Depressive Symptoms
<ul><li>Inflated self-esteem or grandiosity: the unrealistic belief in one's ability, intelligence, and powers; may be delusional; feel like their thoughts are going very fast</li><li>Psychotic features may be present</li><li>Impulsive/Engaging in reckless behavior, despite the likely negative consequences (i.e., lavish spending sprees, giving away possessions, impulsive sexual promiscuity, abuse of alcohol or drugs, reckless driving, or ill-advised business investments</li></ul>	<ul><li>Feeling hopeless and worthless or excessively guilty</li><li>Sleeping either too much or too little</li><li>Loss of interest and enjoyment in activities</li><li>Weight loss or weight gain</li><li>Difficulty concentrating or making decisions</li><li>Frequent thoughts about death or suicide or suicide attempts</li><li>Feeling tired</li></ul>

Restoration in the Valley: A Psychological Resource Manual for Clergy

MOOD DISORDER QUESTIONNAIRE

Name: _____ Date: _____

Instructions: Please answer each question to the best of your ability.

Was there ever a time when…	Yes	No
… you had more energy than usual?	☐	☐
… your thoughts raced so fast you couldn't process your actions properly?	☐	☐
…your hyperactivity led to arguments or trouble?	☐	☐
… you did something unusually foolish or risky?	☐	☐
…you were more sexually active than usual?	☐	☐
…you were easily distracted and couldn't get things done on time?	☐	☐
…the hyperactivity was a threat to your health?	☐	☐
…you talked much faster than usual?	☐	☐
…you had less sleep than usual yet still felt like you had a lot of energy?	☐	☐
…you were spending recklessly?	☐	☐
…the above symptoms were contrasted by periods of inactivity and sadness?	☐	☐
…the above activities were contrasted by lack of interest in anything?	☐	☐
…it was difficult to do any normal activities of living (i.e., showering, eating)?	☐	☐
Do you have any relatives with a history of bipolar disorder or manic-depressive disorder?	☐	☐
Are you taking any medications that are known to affect your mood?	☐	☐
If you said yes to two or more of the above, did they happen to occur at the same time?	☐	☐

If the congregant says **YES** to 8 of the 15 un-shaded questions above **and YES** to the shaded question, you may have a positive screening for a mood disorder. Please make referrals as needed.

Created by Hirschfeld RMA et.al, *American Journal of Psychiatry*, 2000, 157:1873–1875. Used with permission.

THIS INSTRUMENT IS DESIGNED FOR SCREENING PURPOSES ONLY AND IS NOT TO BE USED AS A DIAGNOSTIC TOOL.

End of Section Checklist

- ☐ Complete the assessment
- ☐ If determined that congregant is at risk for suicide, complete suicide screener found in the suicide section of this manual and contact the appropriate emergency psychiatric response team or call 9-1-1
- ☐ Give congregant resources/referrals
- ☐ Offer a message of hope, care, and concern

"God is our refuge and strength. A very present help in in trouble"

PSALM 46:1 (ASV)

BIPOLAR DISORDER RESOURCES

*Los Angeles County Human Services Hotline:
Dial "2-1-1" (24 hours | Bilingual)
https://www.211la.org*

*For LA County Mental Health Agencies, please see
"Los Angeles County Resources" in Appendix A*

NATIONAL RESOURCES

Depression and Bipolar Support Alliance (DBSA)
www.dbsalliance.org
800-826-3632

International Society for Bipolar Disorders
www.isbd.org
412-624-4407

Juvenile Bipolar Research Foundation
www.jbrf.org
914-468-1297

Mental Health America (MHA)
http://www.mentalhealthamerica.net/conditions/bipolar-disorder
800-969-6642

Mood and Anxiety Disorders Institute (MADI) Resource Center
http://www.massgeneral.org/psychiatry/research/resourcelab.aspx?id=15Mental Health America
617-724-5600

National Alliance on Mental Illness (NAMI)
http://www.nami.org/Learn-More/Mental-Health-Conditions/Bipolar-Disorder National
800-950-NAMI

National Suicide Prevention Lifeline
800-273-TALK (8255)
www.suicidepreventionlifeline.org

Psych Central
978-992-0008
https://psychcentral.com/disorders/bipolar/

Ryan Licht Sang Bipolar Foundation
www.ryanlichtsangbipolarfoundation.org
888-944-4408

We Search Together
www.wesearchtogether.org
866-487-0510

SELECTED READING MATERIALS

Bales, J. (2014). *From Bipolar to the Cross—A Real Life Experience of Mental Illness and God's Healing Power.*

Bergen, M. (2008). *A Firm Place to Stand: Finding Meaning in a Life with Bipolar Disorder.*

Copeland, M. E. (1994). *Living without Depression and Manic Depression: A Workbook for Maintaining Mood Stability.*

Fast, J., & Preston, J. (2006). *Take Charge of Bipolar Disorder: A 4-Step Plan for You and Your Loved Ones to Manage the Illness and Create Lasting Stability.*

Fawcett, J., Golden, B., & Rosenfeld, N. (2010). *New Hope for People with Bipolar Disorder.*

Federman, R. (2010). *Facing Bipolar: The Young Adult's Guide to Dealing with Bipolar Disorder.*

Jamison, K. (1997). *An Unquiet Mind: A Memoir of Moods and Madness.*

Miklowitz, D. (2011). *The Bipolar Disorder Survival Guide: What you and your family need to know.*

Peacock, J. (2000). *Bipolar Disorder.*

Smith, H (2010). *Welcome to the Jungle: Everything you ever wanted to know about bipolar but were too freaked out to ask.*

Sylvia, L. (2015). *The Wellness Workbook for Bipolar Disorder: Your Guide to Getting Health and Improving Your Mood.*

White, R. C., & Preston, J. (2009). *Bipolar 101: A Practical Guide to Identifying Triggers, Managing Medications, Coping with Symptoms, and More.*

PART THREE

✓ DOMESTIC VIOLENCE

✓ SUBSTANCE ABUSE

All forms and screening tools can be downloaded on our website under the Resources tab. Go to www.DrValindaB.com and enter the code: RITVtools

DISCLAIMER: THESE CHECKLISTS ARE NOT INTENDED FOR DIAGNOSTIC OR TREATMENT PURPOSES. THEY ARE NOT A SUBSTITUTE FOR ASSESSMENT OR ADVICE FROM A LICENSED PROFESSIONAL.

DOMESTIC VIOLENCE

Domestic violence, which consists of intimate partner violence (IPV), sexual assault, and stalking, is a national epidemic that affects the lives of adults, teens, and children nationwide. The most recent information gathered by the Center for Disease Control in The National Intimate Partner and Sexual Violence Survey of 2010 found that 1 in 4 women and 1 in 7 men have experienced severe physical violence by an intimate partner, and women are disproportionately affected by intimate partner violence, sexual assault, and stalking.[17] According to the Los Angeles Police Department,[18] domestic violence is an abusive criminal offense that occurs between members of the same family or those in a dating relationship. Domestic violence can include physical behaviors such as hitting, shoving, choking, assault with a weapon, and rape (even within the marital relationship), and emotional behaviors such as a pervasive pattern of controlling victim's times and activities, degrading comments, and homicidal and suicidal threats.

Domestic violence is not an isolated event. Rather, it is a cycle or pattern of control and abuse that increases in frequency and intensity over time, resulting in emergency room visits, hospitalizations, and death.[19] The repetitive use of abusive and violent behaviors by perpetrators is utilized to maintain power and control over the victims. These behaviors may include coercion and threats, intimidation, emotional abuse, male privilege, economic abuse, using children, minimizing, denying, blaming, and isolation.[20] While the types and outcomes of domestic violence vary, all domestic violence results in psychological damage. According to a national survey, 81 percent of women and 35 percent of men who experienced rape, stalking, or physical violence by an intimate partner reported significant short-term and long-term symptoms of post-traumatic stress disorder.[21]

The California Partnership to End Domestic Violence[22] shared the results of the California Women's Health Survey of 2010. Approximately 40 percent of California women were expected to experience IPV in their lifetime; women the ages of 18 to 24 were 11 percent more likely to be victims of IPV than women in other age groups; women who had been pregnant in the last five years had higher rates of IPV; and of those who had experienced the IPV, 75 percent had children under the age of 18.

Adult women are not the only group that constitutes a large percentage of domestic violence victims in California. Given the data generated as a result of the 13th Biennial California Student Survey, a survey conducted every two years by 7th, 9th, and 11th grade students, dating violence was reported by 5.4 percent of 9th graders and 11 percent of 11th graders.[23]

Given these alarming statics, clergy will inevitably encounter congregants who have experienced some form of domestic violence. It is imperative that clergy are able to effectively deal with congregants who come to them for assistance. Martin,[24] Murphy,[25] and Miles[26] identified some helpful suggestions in working with victims of domestic violence.

Working with VICTIMS of Domestic Abuse

- Listen to the victim and demonstrate genuine concern
- Reassure the victim that the abuse is not their fault
- Be trustworthy, calm, patient, and respect confidentiality. For example, do not place the victim's name on the prayer list or tell other leaders in the church. This will help to maintain a relationship based on trust and privacy
- Make sure that the victim and the children are safe
- Perpetrators of domestic violence can be manipulative and even charming. Let the victim know that despite the promises, the abuse will likely continue and escalate
- Make it clear that the victim is not alone and that many people experience domestic violence. Also inform them that many victims find it difficult to leave. When normalizing his or her experience, be sure not to minimize his or her feelings
- Encourage the victim to think about a safety plan, which may include setting aside money, making copies of important documents for themselves and the children (i.e., health insurance identification cards, birth certificates, and other important documents, passports, etc.)

- Assure the victim of God's unconditional love and presence, and your commitment to walking with them throughout the process
- Once the victim is safe, help him or her think of long-term life changes
- Continue to pray. Ask God for direction and guidance while working with the victim

Educate yourself. Know about the resources available in your community. A great place to start is The National Domestic Violence Hotline (800-799-7233). Advocates are available 24 hours a day, 7 days a week.

Refrain from:

Making judgments

Losing patience

Attempting to talk to the victim and perpetrator at the same time/offer marital counseling until the batterer receives professional help

Telling the victim they are wrong for wanting to stay

Blaming the victim for the violence

DOMESTIC ABUSE/INTIMATE PARTNER VIOLENCE QUESTIONNAIRE

Name: _____ **Date:** _____

Instructions: Please answer each question to the best of your ability.

Has your spouse/significant other…	Yes	No
Ever refused to do housework or childcare?	☐	☐
Neglected to involve you in important decisions that were supposed to be made together?	☐	☐
Ever been upset with you because things weren't done in the time or way that they wanted it to be (i.e., they were upset that the laundry wasn't done the way they wanted)?	☐	☐
Kept you from doing things that you wanted to do (i.e., spending time with friends)?	☐	☐
Ever stopped you from going to work or school?	☐	☐
Stopped you from having any money for your personal use, or controlled the amount you can have with you at a time?	☐	☐
Said mean or hurtful things to you?	☐	☐
Ever made you do something degrading (i.e., having you ask them for permission to do something or make you beg for something)?	☐	☐
Ever disrespected your time and privacy (i.e., called you repeatedly at work, checked your phone calls or text messages, repeatedly called to know where you are)?	☐	☐
Ever used your children to threaten you (i.e., have they told you that they would harm your children or take them away from you if you did not do as they say)?	☐	☐

Has your spouse/significant other...	Yes	No
Ever told you that you were a bad person, when you are not (i.e., said you were a bad parent)?	☐	☐
Ever said or done any mean and harmful things to you in front of your family and friends?	☐	☐
Ever pressured you to have sex in a way or time that you did not want to?	☐	☐
Ever put your life in danger (i.e., drove dangerously while you were in the car)?	☐	☐
Ever threatened to commit suicide or threaten that something bad would happen if you left them?	☐	☐
Ever pushed, slapped, hit, kicked, manhandled, choked/strangled, punched, grabbed, or shoved you?	☐	☐
Ever threatened to throw something, or throw/used a knife, gun, or other weapon against you?	☐	☐

....
THIS INSTRUMENT IS DESIGNED FOR SCREENING PURPOSES ONLY AND IS NOT TO BE USED AS A DIAGNOSTIC TOOL.
....

The victim is not the only person involved in a domestic violence situation. What if you pastor both victims *and* perpetrators of domestic violence? How do you offer help and guidance for the batterers? Don't they need help, too? Please note that if the victim has already approached you about the violence and you bring it up to the perpetrator, you are likely to increase the risk of endangering the safety of the victim and the children. If the *perpetrator* brings it up to *you*, the following will outline some practical ways to work with them:

Working with PERPETRATORS of Domestic Abuse

- Be clear that violent behavior is unacceptable
- Hold them accountable for their actions. Remember that perpetrators of domestic violence rarely take responsibility for their actions. Rather, they blame substance abuse, the victim, stress, children, and a host of other things for their behavior. Don't accept their rationalizations; don't take their word for it that the violence has stopped, and don't prematurely accept their word that they are a "changed" person. It is your job to hold them accountable
- Protect the safety of the victim and the children by not mentioning any critical information that may increase their risk
- Pray with him or her and answer any spiritual questions they may have. Make it clear that nowhere in the Bible is abusive behavior justified
- Refer him or her to a treatment program designed specifically for perpetrators of domestic violence
- Offer him or her hope that they can change
- Collaborate with community agencies and law enforcement to hold him or her accountable
- Continue to pray. Ask God for direction and guidance while working with the perpetrator

End of Section Checklist

- ☐ Complete the assessment
- ☐ Give congregant resources/referrals
- ☐ Offer a message of hope, care, and concern

"Leave all your worries with Him
because he cares for you"

1 PETER 5:7 (GNT)

DOMESTIC VIOLENCE RESOURCES

*Los Angeles County Human Services Hotline:
Dial "2-1-1" (24 hours | Bilingual)
https://www.211la.org*

*For LA County Mental Health Agencies, please see
"Los Angeles County Resources" in Appendix A*

NATIONAL RESOURCES

National Domestic Violence Hotline
www.thehotline.org
800-799-SAFE (7233)

National Coalition Against Domestic Violence
www.ncadv.org
303-839-1852

National Resource Center on Domestic Violence
www.nrcdv.org
800-537-2238

Futures Without Violence
https://www.futureswithoutviolence.org/engaging-men/programs-for-men-who-use-violence/

Violence Against Women
http://vawnet.org/
800 537-2238

LOS ANGELES COUNTY RESOURCES

Los Angeles LGBT Center Domestic Violence Program
323-860-5806

Los Angeles Rape and Battering Hotline
213-626-3393

LOS ANGELES COUNTY 24-HOUR HOTLINES

Hotlines provide referrals and safety planning for: shelters, legal services, counseling, and more

1736 Family Crisis Center
www.1736familycrisiscenter.org
213-745-6434

Los Angeles County Domestic Violence Hotline
800-978-3600

Los Angeles County Victim Assistance Program
800-380-3811

LOS ANGELES COUNTY SERVICES AND SHELTERS

1736 Family Crisis Center
2116 Arlington Ave.
Los Angeles, CA 90018
www.1736familycrisiscenter.org
213-745-6434

Angel Step Inn
9047 Washington Blvd.

Part Three / Domestic Violence

Pico Rivera, CA 90660
323-780-4357

Center for the Pacific Asian Family
3424 Wilshire Blvd., Suite #1000
Los Angeles, CA 90010
http://nurturingchange.org/
800-339-3940

Chicana Service Action Center
3601 E 1st St.
Los Angeles, CA 90063
800-843-9675

CIFHS-The Family Center
540 S Eremland Dr.
Covina, CA 91723
http://www.cifhs.org/
626-966-1577

Good Shepherd Shelter For Battered Women & Children
http://www.goodshepherdshelter.org/
323-737-6111

Haven Hills
https://www.havenhills.org/contact/
Crisis Line: 818.887.6589

Interval House
6615 E Pacific Coast Hwy # 170,
Long Beach, CA 90803
http://www.intervalhouse.org/
562-594-4555

Jenesse Center, Inc.
3761 Stocker St #100
Los Angeles, CA 90008
https://www.jenesse.org/
800-479-7328

Jewish Family Service of Los Angeles
https://www.jfsla.org/
323-761-8800

Peace Over Violence
1015 Wilshire Blvd.
Los Angeles, CA 90017
http://www.peaceoverviolence.org/
213-955-9090

Rainbow Services
453 W 7th St.
San Pedro, CA 90731
http://www.rainbowservicesdv.org/
310-547-9343

Sojourn Services
https://www.opcc.net/sojourn?nd=sojourn
310-264-6644

Su Casa Family Crisis & Support Center
http://www.sucasadv.org/
3840 Woodruff Ave. Suite 203
Long Beach, CA 90808
24 Hour Hotline: (562) 402-4888

Women Shelter of Long Beach
http://www.womenshelterlb.org/
24 Hour Domestic Violence Hotline: (562) 437-4663

LOS ANGELES COUNTY DOMESTIC VIOLENCE FOR PERPETRATORS TREATMENT PROGRAMS

About Face Domestic Violence Intervention Project
3407 W 6th St #700
Los Angeles, CA 90020
213-384-7084

Open Paths Counseling Center
5731 W. Slauson Ave., Suite 175
Culver City, CA 90230
http://openpaths.org/
310-258-9677 (English)/1-310-967-6090 (Spanish)

SELECTED READING MATERIALS

Baadsgaard, J. (2012). *Healing from Abuse. How the Atonement of Jesus Christ can Heal Broken Hearts and Broken Lives.*

Clark, R. (2005). *Setting the Captives Free.*

Conway, H. (1998). *Domestic Violence and the Church.*

Crippen, J., & Wood, A. (2012). *A Cry For Justice: How the evil of domestic abuse hides in your church.*

Hislop, B. (2010). *Shepherding Women in Pain: Real women, Real issues, and what you need to know to truly help.*

Hunt, J. (2014). *Dysfunctional Family: Making peace with your past.*

Jantz, G. (2009). *Healing the Scars of Emotional Abuse.*

Kroeger, C., & Nason-Clark, N. (2001). *No place for abuse: Biblical and practical resources to counteract domestic violence.*

Lisherness, S. (1997). *Striking Terror No More: The Church responds to domestic violence.*

Martin, G. (2014). "What pastors can do to help the victims of domestic violence in the church." *Enrichment Journal.*

Miles, A. (2000). *Domestic violence: What every pastor needs to know.*

Murphy, N. (2003). *God's reconciling love: A pastor's handbook on domestic violence.*

Nason-Clark, N., Kroeger, C., Fisher-Townsend, B. (2011). *Responding to Abuse in Christian Homes.*

Payne, P. (2015). *Domestic Violence: The awakening of the Church to this important issue in today's society.*

Weatherholt, A. (2008). *Breaking the Silence: The Church responds to domestic violence.*

SUBSTANCE ABUSE

Substance abuse is an epidemic that negatively impacts the physical and emotional health of not only those who engage in it, but the families and children of users and society as a whole as well. According to the Center for Behavioral Health,[27] approximately 27 million Americans over the age of 12 reported using illicit drugs in 2014. An estimated 6.5 million Americans over the age of 12 reported current, non-medical use of prescription drugs, such as painkillers, tranquilizers, stimulants, and sedatives. In 2014, nearly 140 million Americans over the age of 12 were using alcohol, with 16.3 million having reported heavy alcohol use and 60.9 million having reported binge drinking. In 2013, it was reported that 21.5 million Americans age 12 or older met the criteria for a substance use disorder (or addiction), and 22.7 million Americans needed treatment for a substance use disorder, of which only about 2.5 million received such treatment at a specialty facility. Of that 2.5 million, it is estimated that more than 41 percent of those admitted for treatment were for alcohol abuse, 20 percent of admissions were for opiate addiction treatment, and 17 percent were for the treatment of marijuana abuse.[28]

In Los Angeles County,[29] over 60,000 residents were admitted to publically funded substance abuse programs. Drug overdose, including unintentional alcohol poisoning, is the fourth leading cause of death in Los Angeles County; 16.2 percent of adults in Los Angeles County reported binge drinking, and 3.3 percent of adults engaged in heavy drinking. Moreover, drug-related offenses account for the highest percentage of overall felony arrests, and drug use has been found to be prevalent among high school students. In 2012, Brecht30 found that there was a continuing increase in the use of methamphetamines, emerging synthetic drugs, heroin, and prescription opioids. Results derived from data collected from publically funded substance abuse treatment programs identified marijuana, alcohol, heroin, and methamphetamine as the four primary substances used in Los Angeles County. Cocaine accounted for 7 percent of Los Angeles County drug use.[30]

Given the statistics, it is inevitable that clergy will encounter congregants and families who struggle with substance abuse. If the use of substances causes significant impairment or distress in functioning, clergy should help the congregant seek adequate treatment. Symptoms of substance abuse are included below.[31]

Symptoms of Substance Abuse

- Substance is often taken in larger amounts over a long period of time
- Difficult to stop using the substance
- Craving or strong urge to use the substance
- Use causes failure to fulfill home, work, or school obligations
- Withdrawal from family activities or hobbies in order to use substance

- Spending a lot of time obtaining and using the substance, and recovering from its effects
- Inability to stop using a substance despite knowledge of a physical or psychological problem that is worsened by the substance use
- Increased tolerance level (more of the substance is needed to have the desired effect)

When use of the substance stops, symptoms of withdrawal may include:

- Irritability, anger, or aggression
- Nervousness or anxiety
- Difficulty sleeping
- Decreased appetite or weight loss
- Restlessness
- Depressed mood
- Physical symptoms: shakiness, sweating, fever, chills, headache, abdominal pain

Once you identify that drug or alcohol abuse is the source of the problem, Apthorp[32] suggests that clergy should:

- Express warmth and concern for the congregant
- Explain that the emotional distress is a symptom of the substance abuse—the chemicals are the source of the problems, not the result

- Explain that drug abuse or alcoholism is an illness that can be treated
- Offer hope and information about persons who have had successful recovery
- Refer congregant to the appropriate treatment programs in the community

Part Three / Substance Abuse

SUBSTANCE ABUSE SCREENER

Name: _____ **Date:** _____

The term "drug" refers to illegal, prescribed, or over-the-counter substances.

Instructions: Please answer each question to the best of your ability.

	Yes	No
Have you ever used drugs for non-medical reasons?	☐	☐
Have you ever used drugs that were not prescribed to you?	☐	☐
Have you ever used drugs that were prescribed to you, but in a way other than the physician had ordered?	☐	☐
Have you ever used recreational drugs? If so, what kind?	☐	☐
Do you use more than one drug at a time (or drugs & alcohol together)?	☐	☐
Can you get through a week without using drugs/alcohol?	☐	☐
Have you ever "blacked out" or had "visions" as a result of drug or alcohol use?	☐	☐
Do you ever feel guilty about your drug/alcohol use?	☐	☐
Has drugs or alcohol use ever caused familial, marital, or friendship problems?	☐	☐
Have you ever gotten in trouble for drug or alcohol use?	☐	☐
Have you ever thought that you should cut down on your consumption of drugs and/or alcohol?	☐	☐
Have you ever felt bothered by people's comments on the amount of alcohol you consume?	☐	☐

	Yes	No
Do you ever feel guilty about taking drugs or drinking?	☐	☐
Have you ever gone to work under the influence of drugs or alcohol?	☐	☐
Have you ever gotten into a fight while under the influence of drugs or alcohol?	☐	☐
Have you ever done something illegal in order to obtain drugs?	☐	☐
Have you ever had withdrawal symptoms from not having drugs or alcohol?	☐	☐
Have you ever had any medical problems that were a result of drug or alcohol use (convulsions, memory loss, hepatitis, etc.)?	☐	☐
Has someone ever said you needed help with your drug or alcohol use?	☐	☐
Have you ever lost a job due to drug or alcohol use?	☐	☐
Have you ever been arrested for drug use/drug possession or alcohol possession?	☐	☐

End of Section Checklist

- ☐ Complete the assessment
- ☐ Give congregant resources/referrals
- ☐ Offer a message of hope, care, and concern

"The question is not, 'Do you have a problem?'
The question is, does the problem have you?"

JOEL OSTEEN

SUBSTANCE ABUSE RESOURCES

*Los Angeles County Human Services Hotline:
Dial "2-1-1" (24 hours | Bilingual)
https://www.211la.org*

*For LA County Mental Health Agencies, please see
"Los Angeles County Resources" in Appendix A*

NATIONAL RESOURCES

Addiction Center
www.addictioncenter.com
877-655-5116

Alcoholics Anonymous
www.aa.org
212-870-3400

Center on Addiction and the Family
http://www.phoenixhouse.org/family/center-on-addiction-and-the-family/
844-293-7438

Cocaine Anonymous
310-559-5833
www.ca.org

Families Anonymous
www.familiesanonymous.org
800-736-9805

Narcotics Anonymous
www.na.org
818-773-9999 x771

National Association for Children of Alcoholics
www.nacoa.org
301-468-0985

National Institute on Alcohol Abuse & Alcoholism
www.niaaa.nih.gov
301-443-3860

National Council on Alcoholism & Drug Dependence
www.ncadd.org
800-622-2255 (24-Hour Affiliate Referral)

Substance Abuse & Mental Health Services Administration
www.samhsa.gov
877-726-4727

READING MATERIAL

Alcoholics Anonymous. (1992). *Members of the clergy ask about Alcoholics Anonymous.*

Alcoholics Anonymous. Methamphetamine Narcotic. (2016). *Drug Addiction: Substance Abuse: Learn How to Overcome Substance Abuse*

Apthorp, S. (1985). *Alcohol and substance abuse: A clergy handbook.*

Berger, A. (2008). *12 Stupid Things That Mess Up Recovery: Avoiding Relapse through Self-Awareness and Right Action.*

Block, S., Block, C., Du Plessis, G., & Weathers, R. (2016). *Mind-Body Workbook for Addiction: Effective tools for substance-abuse recovery and relapse prevention.*

Kuhn, C., Swartzwelder, S., & Wilson, W. (2014). *Buzzed: The straight facts about the most used and abused drugs from alcohol to ecstasy, 4th Edition.*

Lorenzini, M. (2016). *Drug Addiction Recovery: A guide to take back your life from drug dependency and substance abuse.*

Spiegelman, E. (2015). *Rewired: A bold new approach to addiction and recovery.*

Williams, R. (2012). *The Mindfulness Workbook for Addiction: A guide to coping with the grief, stress and anger that trigger addictive behaviors.*

SELECTED READING MATERIALS FOR LOVED ONES OF ADDICTS

Al-Anon Family Group. (1995). *How Al-Anon works for families and friends of alcoholics.*

Beattie, M. (1992). *Codependent No More: How to Stop Controlling Others and Start Caring for Yourself.*

Bailor, R. (2015). *Chemical Addiction & Family Members.*

Boehnlein-Rice. (2014). *Parent of an Adult Addict: Hope for the broken road.*

Conyers, B. (2009). *Addict In The Family: Stories of loss, hope, and recovery.*

Fossum, M., & Mason, M. (1989). *Facing shame: Families in recovery.* New York, NY: W.W. Norton & Company, Inc.

Miller, A. (2008). *The enabler: When helping hurts the ones you love.* Tucson, AZ: Wheatmark.

Nakken, C. (2010). *Reclaim Your Family from Addiction: How couples and families recover love and meaning.*

Page, K. (2012). *A Parent's Guide to Substance Abuse and Addiction.*

Platter, C. (2009). *Loving an Addict, Loving Yourself: The top 10 survival tips for loving someone with an addiction.*

Rubin, C. (2007). *Don't let your kids kill you: A guide for parents of drug and alcohol addicted children.*

PART FOUR

✓ HOMICIDE PREVENTION

All forms and screening tools can be downloaded on our website under the Resources tab. Go to www. DrValindaB.com and enter the code: RITVtools

DISCLAIMER: THESE CHECKLISTS ARE NOT INTENDED FOR DIAGNOSTIC OR TREATMENT PURPOSES. THEY ARE NOT A SUBSTITUTE FOR ASSESSMENT OR ADVICE FROM A LICENSED PROFESSIONAL.

HOMICIDE PREVENTION

At times, you may encounter congregants who are so overcome with the negative emotions of anger, rage, and revenge that, without having the coping tools to deal with their negative emotions, they may seek vengeance on others. While it is important to create positive and supportive relationships with congregants, it is absolutely imperative to protect them from harming themselves and others. While most communication between clergy and congregants is privileged, there are limits to clergy-congregant confidentiality. Serious intention to commit homicide is one of those limits.

In the famous case Tarasoff v. Regents of the University of California,[33] a client informed his psychotherapist that he was going to kill an unnamed but identifiable woman. Subsequently, the client killed the woman. The parents of the victim sued the regents of the University of California for the therapist's failure to warn the woman or her parents of the danger. In 1985, California legislature instituted the Tarasoff Rule: "California law now provides that a psychotherapist has a duty to protect or warn a third party only if the therapist actually believed or predicted that the patient posed a serious risk of inflicting serious bodily injury upon a reasonably identifiable victim."[34] This is referred to as **duty to warn.**

While members of the clergy are not psychotherapists, they are privy to certain confidential information that requires them to protect congregants and potential victims. Thus, if a member of the clergy who is in an ongoing counseling relationship reasonably believes that the congregant may commit a dangerous crime, they are obligated to warn potential victims and law enforcement of potential physical violence.[35,36] Clergy should only reveal information that is necessary to prevent danger to others.

Not only is it important to warn potential victims of impending danger, but Herman[37] suggested that members of clergy institute a **second duty to warn**. That is, clergy must clearly communicate the harmful disposition of the congregant's intended course of action.[38] For example, just as a medical doctor tells a patient the side effects of a certain medication or the contagious nature of a disease, clergy should tell congregants about the consequences of their intended actions. The second duty to warn is not mandatory, but is strongly advised.

If during a counseling relationship a congregant says, "I am going to kill [X]," it is your duty to warn the potential victim and contact authorities. However, if the congregant says, "I am going to kill again," the clergy member should only institute the second duty to warn, as there is no identifiable person or persons who may be harmed.

What to do with a homicidal congregant

- Advise the congregant about the consequences of their actions
- Contact law enforcement or dial 9-1-1
- If the victim(s) are identifiable, warn the victim(s) of the potential danger

- Refer congregant to community mental health resources that can assist them in developing appropriate coping and communication skills
- Document the conversation and interventions that you implemented

How to inform intended victims

*Adapted from Merrill[39]

- Immediately attempt to reach the intended victim by phone, certified letter, or e-mail. If sending a certified letter, it can be delivered next day or by hand to last known address
- You may only disclose information deemed "absolutely necessary." This includes the specific threat or plan, who has issued the threat, its immediate context, previously known history of violence if it relates to the current threat, and the clergy member's reason for determining its seriousness
- If you are unable to reach the intended victim by phone or other means, contact law enforcement so they can attempt to notify the intended victim
- You may send a certified, next-day letter, or hand deliver a letter, to the last known address

Restoration in the Valley: A Psychological Resource Manual for Clergy

HOMICIDE RISK ASSESSMENT

Name: _____ Date: _____

Instructions: Administer this assessment verbally and record responses. Do not give the checklist to the congregant.

	Yes	No
Have you ever been so angry you wanted to hurt someone?	☐	☐
Have you ever felt that the only way to make someone do what you want is through force/aggression?	☐	☐
Do you have difficulty finding hope in life?	☐	☐
Have you ever planned to hurt someone? (If yes, ask how.)	☐	☐
Have you ever had thoughts of suicide?	☐	☐
Have you ever attempted to kill yourself or participated in self-harming behaviors?	☐	☐
Have you experienced any recent loss or crises?	☐	☐
If you decided to hurt _____, how would you do it? What plans have you made?	☐	☐
If you were ready to carry out your plan to harm _____, what methods would you use?	☐	☐
What things or people can you think of that might stop you from trying to hurt_____?	☐	☐
What would be some of the consequences of your actions?	☐	☐

*Adapted from Merrill, G. (2013). "Assessing client dangerousness to self and others: Stratified risk management approaches." *Berkeley Social Welfare*.

THIS INSTRUMENT IS DESIGNED FOR SCREENING PURPOSES ONLY AND IS NOT TO BE USED AS A DIAGNOSTIC TOOL.

End of Section Checklist

- ☐ Complete the assessment
- ☐ Inform law enforcement
- ☐ Attempt to inform potential victim and document your efforts
- ☐ Implement second duty to warn
- ☐ Give congregant resources/referrals
- ☐ Offer a message of hope, care, and concern

"Every day we have plenty of opportunities to get angry, stressed or offended. But what you're doing when you indulge in these negative emotions is giving something outside yourself power over your happiness. You can choose to not let little things upset you."

JOEL OSTEEN

HOMICIDE PREVENTION RESOURCES

*Los Angeles County Human Services Hotline:
Dial "2-1-1" (24 hours | Bilingual)
https://www.211la.org*

*For LA County Mental Health Agencies, please see
"Los Angeles County Resources" in Appendix A*

Contact law enforcement or dial 9-1-1

SELECTED READING MATERIALS

Herman, M. (n.d.). The Liability of Clergy for the Acts of Their Congregants. *Georgetown Law Journal.* 98(1). http://georgetownlawjournal.org/files/pdf/98-1/Herman.PDF

Milne, T. (1986). Bless Me Father for I Am About to Sin...: Should Clergy Counselors Have a Duty to Protect Third Parties? *Tulsa Law Review.* 22(2). http://digitalcommons.law.utulsa.edu/cgi/viewcontent.cgi?article=1762&context=tlr

Schaefer, A., & Levine, D. (1996). No Sanctuary From the Law: Legal issues facing clergy. *Loyola of Los Angeles Law Review.* 30(1).

PART FIVE

CHILD ABUSE:

- ✓ MANDATED REPORTING
- ✓ SEXUAL ABUSE
- ✓ PHYSICAL ABUSE, EMOTIONAL ABUSE
- ✓ NEGLECT

All forms and screening tools can be downloaded on our website under the Resources tab. Go to www.DrValindaB.com and enter the code: RITVtools

DISCLAIMER: THESE CHECKLISTS ARE NOT INTENDED FOR DIAGNOSTIC OR TREATMENT PURPOSES. THEY ARE NOT A SUBSTITUTE FOR ASSESSMENT OR ADVICE FROM A LICENSED PROFESSIONAL.

CHILD ABUSE

Child abuse is an epidemic that impacts children all over the world. Childhelp,[40] an organization devoted to the prevention and treatment of child abuse, reported the following national statistics:

- A report of child abuse is made every ten seconds
- More than four children die every day as a result of child abuse
- It is estimated that between 50 and 60 percent of child fatalities due to maltreatment are not recorded as such on death certificates
- Approximately 70 percent of children who die from abuse are under the age of four
- More than 90 percent of juvenile sexual abuse victims know their perpetrator in some way
- Child abuse occurs at every socioeconomic level, across ethnic and cultural lines, within all religions, and at all levels of education
- About 30 percent of abused and neglected children will later abuse their own children, continuing the horrible cycle of abuse
- In at least one study, about 80 percent of 21-year-olds who were abused as children met criteria for at least one psychological disorder

In Los Angeles County, the Department of Children and Family Services (DCFS) conducts approximately 150,000 child safety investigations each year.[41]

In 2015, over 200,000 calls were made to the County of Los Angeles DCFS child protection hotline and over 150,000 child safety investigations were conducted. Of the 35,000 children receiving continuing (monthly) services, 18,000 are in foster care.

Whether the abuse is physical, emotional, sexual, or neglect, the psychological impact can be severe. As a member of the clergy, you will undoubtedly be exposed to child abuse either through report or direct observation. People will seek your counsel, and sometimes you will be asked to keep certain situations a secret. However, the reality is that not reporting suspected or actual child abuse is against the law, as you are **legally mandated** to make a report to authorities.

Reporting child abuse can be an emotion-provoking process. You may worry about your relationship with the family and the suspect, and have distressing doubts about how the family will react; you may wonder about the outcome, and whether or not the report will put the child at more risk. These concerns are valid. However, if you think of reporting child abuse as an **intervention** for the family and as part of your role as an advocate for the child, it may help to change your perspective and make reporting more bearable. In this section, you will gain insight into your role as a mandated reporter, and how and when to report. Hopefully this information will make you better prepared for the reporting process.

MANDATED REPORTING

REPORTING LAWS REGARDING MINORS

What is a mandated reporter?

Mandated reporters are individuals who are mandated by law to report known or suspected child maltreatment. They are primarily people who have contact with children through their employment, such as school nurses or day care providers. Mandated reporters are required by law to report any known or suspected instances of child abuse or neglect to an appropriate agency, such as child protective services, a local law enforcement agency (local police/sheriff's department), or your state's toll-free child abuse reporting hotline. For assistance with filing a report and for child abuse resources, call **1-800-4-A-CHILD (1-800-422-4453) or visit www.childhelp.org.**

Are clergy required to report child abuse?

Yes. While procedures and privileged communication requirements may vary from state to state, every state has statutes requiring clergy to report child maltreatment. For example, in the state of California and under the Child Abuse and Neglect Reporting Act, mandated reporters include a clergy member; "...a priest, minister, rabbi, religious practitioner, or similar functionary of a church, temple, or recognized denomination or organization" (PC 11165.7 (a)(32)) and any custodian of records of a clergy member. For more specific information about your state's mandated reporting laws, contact Child Welfare Information Gateway at 800-394-3366, visit their website https://www.childwelfare.gov/pubPDFs/clergymandated.pdf, or consult legal counsel.

Isn't there some sort of privacy or privilege as it relates to the clergy/congregant relationship?

Clergy-penitent privilege is the recognition of the right to maintain confidential communication between professionals and their clients, patients, or congregants. This means that clergy are not obligated to disclose confidential communication in a court proceeding. This privilege is intended to protect the congregant. While there is such a thing as clergy-penitent privilege, it "does not modify or limit the clergy member's duty to report known or suspected child abuse or neglect when the clergy member is acting in some other capacity that would otherwise make the clergy member a mandated reporter."[42] What this means is that when a member of clergy knows of or has reasonable suspicion that child abuse has occurred, they have a legal obligation to report it.

Why is reporting important?

Children are helpless, and are in need of loving and trustworthy adult advocates who support them. While you cannot submit an anonymous report as a mandated reporter, your identity will not be disclosed to the family or anyone else not directly involved in the case. If the case goes to trial and you are required to testify, your identity may be revealed. Keep in mind that in the event that a case goes to trial, your testimony may be essential in protecting the child. Take action! **Reporting child abuse *is* an intervention. You could save a child's life.**

When do you report?

If a mandated reporter, in his or her professional capacity, or within the scope of his or her employment, has knowledge of or observes a child whom the reporter knows or reasonably suspects is the victim of abuse or neglect, it must be reported.[43] Note that the law states that a mandated reporter needs to have **reasonable suspicion** of abuse or neglect. What that means is that you do not need **proof** of abuse, only the **suspicion** that the abuse has occurred in order to report. Your job is not to be the investigator; rather, a reporter. Your local child protection agency and law enforcement will conduct an investigation.

Oftentimes children will make statements such as, "I will tell you only if you can keep a secret." You cannot make this promise. Remember, you are a mandated reporter, and child abuse is one of the reasons to break confidentiality. If you lie to the child and they find out later that you reported the abuse, you may harm the relationship. Be sure to remind the child that you are there to keep them safe, and that means finding them the proper help.

Without clear, hard evidence that a child has been abused (i.e., bruises, direct observation of abuse, verbal report), it may be difficult to determine when a member of clergy should submit a child abuse report. It is imperative that clergy look for indicators of abuse and rely on experience when with children and families to determine whether or not a report should be made.[44] Signs and symptoms of the different types of child abuse will be outlined later in this section. *If you are unsure whether something is reportable, call your local Child Protection Hotline. Counselors and advisors are available 24 hours a day, 7 days a week.*

How do you report?

You must make a report immediately (or within 36 hours) by phone to the identified child abuse reporting agency or law enforcement agency. If you are unsure of whom to contact, call the 24/7 Childhelp National Child Abuse Hotline at 1-800-4-A-Child (1-800-422-4453). To report child abuse in Los Angeles County, contact the Department of Child and Family Services (DCFS) Child Protection Hotline, 24 hours a day, 7 days a week at (800) 540-4000. In case of an emergency, immediately call 9-1-1.

In California, a written report must be forwarded within 36 hours of receiving the information regarding the incident. The written report must be filed on Department of Justice Form SS 8572 (DOJ SS 8572), known as the Suspected Child Abuse Report Form. This form is available through the DCFS website (http://dcfs.co.la.ca.us/contactus/childabuse.html), local law enforcement agencies or, in some instances, county probation departments.

Here is some of the information you will need when making a child abuse report:

- The demographics of the victim (name, address, phone number, etc.)
- Sibling information (this is important when intervening on behalf of the other children in the home as well)
- Parent/Guardian information
- Suspect information
- Description of the incident

What happens if I don't report?

Reporting child abuse can be difficult and anxiety producing. It becomes increasingly difficult for clergy who are close to the family members involved in a child abuse claim. While this is understandable, failure to report is considered a misdemeanor punishable by up to six months in jail and/or fines. You may also be subject to a civil lawsuit.

Reporting child abuse is not an option for clergy—it is mandatory. If you think of reporting as a form of intervention, protection, and advocacy, it may help to reduce some of the feelings of fear and other emotional reactions associated with reporting.

Risk Factors for Child Abuse

The following are some risk factors for child abuse:

- Domestic violence
- Substance abuse
- Poverty
- Lack of parenting skills
- Untreated mental illness of parent
- Stress and lack of support
- Chronic illness

SEXUAL ABUSE

Child sexual abuse is defined as any form of non-consensual sexual activity that was coerced or in any other way not voluntary, between an adult and a child. Sexual activity is any activity that is meant to sexually arouse the child or adult, or to exploit the child.[45]

Examples of this include intercourse, masturbation, oral and anal sex, kissing, touching, fondling, groping (even through clothing), or showing pornography.

There are two occasions where sexual activity of a minor is reportable: (1) sexual abuse and (2) the age difference between the child and their partner.

Physical Signs of Sexual Abuse

- Bruising tearing, pain, itching, or bleeding around genital area, including rectum
- Difficulty walking or sitting
- Swelling or discharge from vagina/penis
- An STD or pregnancy, especially under the age of 14
- Visible lesions around mouth and genitals
- Complaint of lower abdominal pain
- Painful urination, defecation
- Yeast infections

Behavioral Signs of Abuse:

- Sexualized behavior or promiscuity
- Displays knowledge of or interest in sexual acts inappropriate for their age and development
- Makes strong efforts to avoid a particular person without an obvious reason
- Hostility or aggression
- Fearfulness or withdrawn behavior
- Self-injurious behaviors
- Nightmares or bedwetting
- Running away from home
- Alcoholism/drug abuse
- Signs of depression or post-traumatic stress disorder
- Difficulty in school, such as a decrease in grades and attendance

The difference between the age of the child and partner is also a factor in determining whether or not to report. This has to do with **consensual** sexual activity. The following chart outlines when it is necessary to make a report.

	Age of partner										
Age of child		12	13	14	15	16	17	18	19	20	21	22+
	11	N	N	Y	Y	Y	Y	Y	Y	Y	Y	Y
	12	N	N	Y	Y	Y	Y	Y	Y	Y	Y	Y
	13	N	N	Y	Y	Y	Y	Y	Y	Y	Y	Y
	14	Y	Y	N	N	N	N	N	N	N	Y	Y
	15	Y	Y	N	N	N	N	N	N	N	Y	Y
	16	Y	Y	N	N	N	N	N	N	N	N	N
	17	Y	Y	N	N	N	N	N	N	N	N	N
	18	Y	Y	N	N	N	N	N	N	N	N	N
	19	Y	Y	N	N	N	N	N	N	N	N	N
	20	Y	Y	N	N	N	N	N	N	N	N	N
	21+	Y	Y	Y	Y	N	N	N	N	N	N	N

Chart adapted by David Knopf, LCSW, UCSF (2002)

*Chart created by David Knopf, LCSW, UCSF (2002). National Center for Youth Law. Jul. 2004. No permission required.

PHYSICAL & EMOTIONAL ABUSE, NEGLECT

PHYSICAL ABUSE

Physical abuse is defined as "any injury caused deliberately that intentionally discounts the health and safety of a child or that results in psychological damage."[46]

According to the Child Abuse and Neglect Reporting Act, an injury is defined as a traumatic condition and includes serious harm such as burns, cuts, broken bones, welts, severe bruises, or scars. This also includes unlawful corporal punishment such a beatings using a belt that leaves scars.[47]

Some physical and behavioral signs are listed below.

Physical Signs of Abuse (not an exhaustive list)

- Unexplained injuries like fractures, bruises, or lacerations
- Bruises and welts appearing on the bottom, face, genitals, or back
- Burns or scalds
- Abdominal, head, or brain injuries
- Bite marks
- Injury to a young baby or infant

Behavioral Signs of Abuse

- Hostile or aggressive behavior
- Extreme fear or withdrawn behavior
- Is "on alert," as if they are waiting for something bad to happen
- Violence to animals or other children
- Afraid to go home
- Shies away from touch

- Destructiveness
- Flinches at sudden movements
- Verbal aggression
- Wears inappropriate clothing to cover up injuries, such as long-sleeved shirts in the summer

EMOTIONAL ABUSE

Emotional abuse can severely damage a child's social development and mental health, resulting in psychological harm. It can include constant belittling, shaming, and humiliation; name calling; frequent yelling, threatening, or bullying; exposing a child to violence or the abuse of others; limited emotional contact with the child; and ignoring or rejecting a child as punishment.

Signs of Emotional Abuse

- Lacks self-esteem; constant negative self-talk
- Excessively withdrawn, fearful, or anxious about doing something wrong
- Does not seem to be attached to caregiver
- Constantly seeks approval
- Takes on the role as caregiver to other children or becomes infantile (i.e., thumb sucking, rocking, tantrums)
- Inability to be autonomous (i.e., inability to make choices independently, fears rejection)
- Hostile, verbally abusive, provocative

NEGLECT

Neglect can be defined as risking, causing, or permitting the health of a child to be seriously endangered by intentionally failing to provide adequate food, clothing, shelter, or medical care.[48] There are two types of neglect: Severe neglect and general neglect. Severe neglect refers to the failure of a caregiver to protect the child from grave malnutrition, withholding necessary medical treatment, or willfully placing the child's health in danger. General neglect refers to the negligent failure of a caregiver to provide a child with adequate food, shelter, clothing, medical care, or supervision, where no physical injury to the child has occurred.

Physical Signs of Neglect

- Malnutrition or poorly balanced diet (i.e., extremely thin, pale, dry, flaking skin, fainting)
- Inappropriate dress for the weather (i.e., shorts in the winter)
- Extremely offensive body odor
- Dirty, unkempt
- Unattended or untreated medical conditions

Behavioral Signs of Neglect

- Clingy or indiscriminate attachment
- Self-imposed isolation
- Depression or passivity
- Frequently left unsupervised or allowed to play in

dangerous environments
- Frequently late to school or excessive absences

End of Section Checklist

- ☐ Complete the assessment
- ☐ Document
- ☐ Contact the proper authorities
- ☐ Complete a child abuse report over the phone
- ☐ Submit a written report online within 36 hours

"He will wipe every tear from their eyes,
and there will be no more death or sorrow or
crying or pain. All things are gone forever."

REVELATION 21:4 (NLT)

CHILD ABUSE RESOURCES

*Los Angeles County Human Services Hotline:
Dial "2-1-1" (24 hours | Bilingual)
https://www.211la.org*

*For LA County Mental Health Agencies, please see
"Los Angeles County Resources" in Appendix A*

**To report child abuse in LA County, contact the
Department of Children and Family Services at
800-540-4000**

NATIONAL RESOURCES

For resources and information regarding child abuse laws for each state, and for crises assistance and other counseling referral services, contact:

Child Welfare Information Gateway
https://www.childwelfare.gov/topics/responding/reporting/how/
Hotline (24 hours a day, 7 days a week): 800-422-4453

American Academy of Child and Adolescent Psychiatry
http://www.aacap.org/aacap/Families_and_Youth/Resource_Centers/Child_Abuse_Resource_Center/Home.aspx

Childhelp
www.childhelp.org
480-922-8212

Child Molestation Research & Prevention Institute
http://www.childmolestationprevention.org
510-740-1410

National Children's Advocacy Center
http://www.nationalcac.org/
256-533-5437

National Children's Alliance
http://www.nationalchildrensalliance.org/
202-548-0090

National Parent Helpline
http://www.nationalparenthelpline.org/
855-427-2736

North American Resource Center for Child Welfare
http://www.narccw.com/
614-251-6000

National Child Traumatic Stress Network
http://www.nctsn.org/
(310) 235-2633

Prevent Child Abuse America
http://preventchildabuse.org
312-663-3520

Stop it Now!
http://www.stopitnow.org/
413.587.3500

The American Professional Society on the Abuse of Children
https://www.apsac.org

HOTLINES

Childhelp National Child Abuse Hotline
800-422-4453

Department of Children Family Services (Los Angeles County)
213-351-5507

National Parent Helpline (emotional support and resources for parents)
855-427-2736

PARENT RESOURCES

Parents Anonymous
www.parentsanonymous.org
855-427-2736

Parents Helping Parents
www.parentshelpingparents.org

Parental Stress Line (24 hours a day, 7 days a week)
800-632-8188

Strategies 2.0
www.familyresourcecenters.net
844-359-7684

SELECTED READING MATERIALS

Allender, D. (2016). *Healing the Wounded Heart: The heartache of sexual abuse and the hope of transformation.*

Anderson, B. (1992). *When child abuse comes to church.* Minneapolis, MN: Bethany House.

Caldwell, B. (2004). *Safe Kids: Policies & procedures for protecting children in the Church.*

Glover, V. (2005). *Protecting Your Church Against Sexual Predators: Legal FAQs for Church leaders.*

Hammar, R., Klipowicz, S., & Cobble, J. (1993). *Reducing the Risk of Child Sexual Abuse in Your Church: A complete and practical guidebook for prevention and risk reduction.*

Heirtritter, L., & Vought, J. (2006). *Helping Victims of Sexual Abuse: A sensitive biblical guide for counselors, victims, and families.*

Jantz, G. (2009). *Healing the Scars of Emotional Abuse.*

Matthews, D. (2012). *Sexual Abuse of Power in the Black Church: Sexual misconduct in the African American churches.*

McGlone, G., Shrader, M., & Delgatto, L. (2003). *Creating Safe and Sacred Places: Identifying, preventing, and healing sexual abuse.*

Melton, T. (2008). *Safe Sanctuaries: Reducing the risk of abuse in the Church for children and youth.*

Reju, D. (2014). *On Guard: Preventing and responding to child abuse at Church.*

Townsend, D. (2013). *Child Abuse and the Church.*

Zarra, E. (1997). *It Should Never Happen Here: A guide for minimizing the risk of child abuse in ministry.*

APPENDIX A

Los Angeles Mental Health Agencies Divided by spa (area)

Los Angeles County Human Services Hotline: Dial "2-1-1" (24 hours | Bilingual)
https://www.211la.org

ANTELOPE VALLEY

American Health Services - El Dorado Community Service Centers
2720 E. Palmdale Blvd., Ste. 128-129
Palmdale, CA 93550
www.americanhealthservices.org
661-947-3333

Children's Bureau
44226 10th St.
Lancaster, CA 93534
www.all4kids.org
661-471-8575

Children's Bureau
1529 E. Palmdale Blvd., Ste. 210
Palmdale, CA 93534
www.all4kids.org
661-272-9996

Child and Family Guidance Center
40005 10th St. West, Ste. 106

Palmdale, CA 93551
www.childguidance.org
661-265-8627

Hathaway-Sycamores
44738 Sierra Hwy.
Lancaster, CA 93534
www.hathaway-sycamores.org
661-942-5749

Heritage Clinics - Palmdale
1037 W. Avenue N, Ste. 205
Palmdale, CA 93551
www.centerforagingresources.org
661-575-9365

Mental Health America of Los Angeles - Antelope Valley
506 W. Jackman St.
Lancaster, CA 93534
www.mhala.org
661-726-2850

Mental Health America of Los Angeles- Antelope Valley
1609 E. Palmdale Blvd., Ste. G
Palmdale, CA 93550
www.mhala.org
661-947-1595

Optimist Outpatient Mental Health
520 Palmdale Blvd., Units D-F
Palmdale, CA 93551
www.oyhfs.org

Palmdale Mental Health Center
1529 E. Palmdale Blvd., Ste. 150
Palmdale, CA 93550
www.dmh.lacounty.gov
661-575-1800

Tarzana Treatment Centers- Antelope Valley
44443 N. 10th St. West
Lancaster, CA 93534
www.tarzanatc.org
661-726-2630

Veterans Administration Greater Los Angeles Health care System
340 E Avenue I, Suite 108
Lancaster, CA 93534
www.losangeles.va.gov
661-729-8655

Year Round Shelter Program
43423 Division St.
Lancaster, CA 93535
661-945-7524

CENTRAL/METRO LOS ANGELES

About Face: Domestic Violence Intervention Project
3407 W. 6th St., Ste. 700
Los Angeles, CA 90020
www.aboutface-dvip.com
213-384-7084

AIDS Project Los Angeles
611 S. Kingsley Dr.
Los Angeles, CA 90005

www.apla.org
866-772-2365

All Peoples Community Center
822 E. 20th St.
Los Angeles, CA 90011
www.allpeoplescc.org
213-747-6357 23

Amanecer Community Counseling Service
1200 Wilshire Blvd., Ste. 210
Los Angeles, CA 90017
www.amanecerla.org
213-482-9400

Augustus Hawkins
1720 E. 120th St.
Los Angeles, CA 90059
310-668-4272

Aviva Family and Children's Services
7120 Franklin Ave
Los Angeles, CA 90046
323-876-0550

Behavioral Health Services
4099 N. Mission Rd.
Los Angeles, CA 90032
www.bhs-inc.org
323-221-1746

Bienvenidos Children's Center
316 W. 2nd St., Ste. 800
Los Angeles, CA 90012

www.bienvenidos.org
213-785-5906

California Hispanic Commission on Alcohol and Drug Abuse (CHCADA)
530 N. Avenue 54
Los Angeles, CA 90042
www.chcada.org
323-254-2423

California Hospital Medical Center-California Behavioral Health Clinic
1400 S. Grand Ave., Ste. 600
Los Angeles, CA 90015
www.hopestreetfamilycenter.org
213-742-6250

Children's Institute
2121 W. Temple St.
Headquarters - Otis Booth Campus
Los Angeles, CA 90026
www.childrensinstitute.org
213-260-7600

Children's Institute Inc.
711 South New Hampshire Avenue
Los Angeles, CA 90057
213-385-5100

Clinica Monsenor Oscar A. Romero Community Health Center
123 S. Alvarado St.
Los Angeles, CA 90057
www.clinicaromero.com
213-989-7700

Coalition of Mental Health Professionals
9219 S. Broadway
Los Angeles, CA 90003
www.mentalhealthprofessionals.org

El Centro Del Pueblo
1157 Lemoyne St.
Los Angeles, CA 90026
www.ecdp.simplesend.com
213-483-6335

Enki East LA
2523 West 7th Street
Los Angeles, CA 90057
213-480-1557

Enki Youth and Family Services - Boyle Heights
560 S. St. Louis St.
Los Angeles, CA 90033
www.ehrs.com
866-227-1302

Heritage Clinic (Senior Services)
155 N. Occidental Blvd., Ste. 243
Los Angeles, CA 90026
www.centerforagingresources.org
213-382-4400

Hillsides Family Resource
1910 W. Sunset Blvd., Ste. 650
Los Angeles, CA 90026
www.hillsides.org
213-201-5380

Appendix A

Hollygrove
815 North El Centro Avenue
Los Angeles, CA 90038
323-463-2119

Homeless Health Care Los Angeles
512 E. 4th St.
Los Angeles, CA 90013
www.hhcla.org
213-744-0724

Jewish Family Service of Los Angeles
3580 Wilshire Blvd., Ste. 700
Los Angeles, CA 90010
www.jfsla.org
877-275-4537

JWCH Institute
5650 Jillson St.
Commerce, CA 90040
www.jwchinstitute.org
323-201-4516

Kendren Community Mental Health Services
4211 Avalon Blvd
Los Angeles, CA 90011
323-233-0425

LAMP Community
(Homeless Services)
627 San Julian St.
Los Angeles, CA 90014
www.lampcommunity.org
213-488-0031

Los Angeles Centers for Alcohol and Drug Abuse
470 E. Third St., #A, #B
Los Angeles, CA 90013
www.lacada.com
213-626-6411

Los Angeles Child Guidance Clinic
4401 S. Crenshaw Blvd., Ste. 300
Los Angeles, CA 90043
www.lacgc.org
323-290-8360

Los Angeles Child Guidance Clinic
3787 S. Vermont Ave.
Los Angeles, CA 90007
www.lacgc.org
323-766-2345

Los Angeles Christian Health Centers
311 Winston St.
Los Angeles, CA 90013
www.lachc.com
213-893-1960

Magnolia Place Family Center
1910 Magnolia Ave.
Los Angeles, CA 90007
www.all4kids.org
888-255-4543

Mental Health Advocacy Services
3255 Wilshire Blvd., Ste. 902
Los Angeles, CA 90010

www.mhas-la.org
213-389-2077

Mt. Carmel Treatment Center
801 W. 70th St.
Los Angeles, CA 90044
323-759-0340

NAMI-South Central
1773 E. Century Blvd.
Los Angeles, CA 90002
www.namica.org
310-668-4271

New Directions for Veterans
11303 Wilshire Blvd.
VA Building #116
Los Angeles, CA 90073
www.NDvets.org
310-914-5966

Northeast Family Mental Health Service
5321 Via Marisol Street
Los Angeles, CA 90064
323-478-8200

Para Los Ninos
838 E. 6th St.
Los Angeles, CA 90021
www.paralosninos.org
213-623-8446

Penny Lane Centers
2450 South Atlantic Blvd #100

Commerce, CA 90040
323-318-9960

Portals
2500 Wilshire Blvd., Ste. 500
Los Angeles, CA 90057
www.portalshouse.org
213-639-0299

Project Return Peer Support Network
2677 Zoe Ave., Ste. 303A
Huntington Park, CA 90255
www.prpsn.org
323-312-0640

Prototypes
1000 N. Alameda St., Ste. 390
Los Angeles, CA 90012
www.prototypes.org
213-542-3838

Quality Parenting
4909 St. Louis Ct.
Culver City, CA 90230
www.qualityparenting.com
310-839-1571

San Antonio Mental Health Center
2629 Clarendon Ave., 2nd Fl.
Huntington Park, CA 90255
www.dmh.lacounty.gov
323-584-3700

Share!
425 S. Broadway
Los Angeles, CA 90013
www.shareselfhelp.org
213-213-0100

Shields for Families
9624 Compton Ave.
Los Angeles, CA 90002
www.shieldsforfamilies.org
323-568-2055

Shields for Families
12021 S. Wilmington Ave.
Lot C
Los Angeles, CA 90059
www.shieldsforfamilies.org
323-242-5000

Skid Row Housing Trust
647 S. San Pedro St.
Los Angeles, CA 90014
323-541-1411

Social Model Recovery System Inc.- Mid Valley
453 S. Indiana St.
Los Angeles, CA 90063
www.socialmodelrecovery.org
323-266-7725

South Central Health & Rehab
5201 S. Vermont Avenue
Los Angeles, CA 90037
323-751-2677

Southern California Counseling Center
5615 West Pico Boulevard
Los Angeles, CA 90019
323-937-1344

Special Service for Groups
1665 W. Adams Blvd.
Los Angeles, CA 90007
844-422-5577
www.ssg.org

Soledad Enrichment Action, Inc.
735 S. Soto St.
Los Angeles, CA 90023
www.seacharter.org
323-262-8506

St. Anne's Residential Facility
155 N. Occidental Blvd.
Los Angeles, CA 90026
www.stannes.org
213-381-2931

St. John's Child and Family Center
1910 Magnolia Ave.
Los Angeles, CA 90007
www.wellchild.org
213-749-0947

Tessie Cleveland Community Service Corporation
8019 S. Compton Ave.
Los Angeles, CA 90001
www.tccsc.org
323-586-7333

United Friends of the Children
1055 Wilshire Blvd., Ste. 1955
Los Angeles, CA 90017
www.unitedfriends.org
213-580-1850

Violence Intervention Project
1721 Griffin Ave.
Los Angeles, CA 90031
www.violenceinterventionprogram.org
323-221-4134

WLCAC Homeless Access Center
958 E. 108th St.
Los Angeles, CA 90059
www.wlcac.org
323-563-4721

GATEWAY CITIES

Alma Family Services
18780 Amar Rd., Ste. 204
Walnut, CA 91789
www.almafamilyservices.org
323-881-3799

American Health Services
21505 Norwalk Blvd.
Hawaiian Gardens, CA 90716
www.americanhealthservices.org
562-916-7581

American Indian Counseling Center
17707 Studebaker Rd., #208

Cerritos, CA 90703
562-402-0677

Biola Counseling Center
12625 La Mirada Blvd., Ste. 202
La Mirada, CA 90638
www.biolacounselingcenter.com
562-903-4800

Community Family Guidance Center
10929 South St., Ste. 208-B
Cerritos, CA 90703
www.cfgcenter.com
562-924-5526

David and Margaret Youth and Family Services
1350 3rd St.
La Verne, CA 91750
www.dmhome.org
909-596-5921

Enki Health and Research Systems
6001 Clara St.
Bell Gardens, CA 90201
www.ehrs.com
562-806-5000

Family Service of Pomona Valley
436 W. 4th St., Ste. 215
Pomona, CA 91766
909-620-1776

For the Child
4001 Long Beach Blvd.

Long Beach, CA 90807
www.forthechild.org
562-427-7671

Guidance Center
1301 Pine Ave.
Long Beach, CA 90813
www.tgclb.org
562-595-1159

Helpline Youth Counseling Inc.
12440 E. Firestone Blvd., Ste. 1000
Norwalk, CA 90650
www.hycinc.org
562-864-3722

La Casa Mental Health Rehab Center
(Serious Mental Illness)
6060 North Paramount Blvd
Long Beach, CA 90805
562-634-9534

Leroy Haynes Center
233 W. Baseline Rd.
La Verne, CA 91750
www.leroyhaynes.org
909-593-2581

Los Angeles Centers for Alcohol and Drug Abuse
11015 Bloomfield
Santa Fe Springs, CA 90670
562-906-2676

McKinley Children's Center
762 W. Cypress St.
San Dimas, CA 91773
www.mckinleycc.org
909-599-1227

Mental Health Urgent Care Center at Long Beach
6060 Paramount Blvd.
Long Beach, CA 90805
www.telecarecorp.com
562-790-1860

NAMI California
462 N. Indian Hill Blvd, Ste. A
Claremont, CA 91711
www.namica.org
909-399-0305

Pacific Clinics El Camino
11721 Telegraph Rd.
Santa Fe Springs, CA 90670
www.pacificclinics.org
877-722-2737

Palm House
2515 E. Jefferson St.
Carson, CA 90810
310-830-7803

Providence Community Services
11745 Firestone Blvd.
Norwalk, CA 90650
562-207-4272

Appendix A

Straight Talk, Inc.
5712 Camp St.
Cypress, CA 90630
www.straighttalkcounseling.org
714-828-2000

Support for Harbor Area Women's Lives
936 S. Centre St.
San Pedro, CA 90731
310-521-9310
www.shawlwomenshouse.org

Tavarua Health Services
8207 Whittier Blvd.
Pico Rivera, CA 90660
562-695-0737

Whole Child Mental Health and Housing Services
10155 Colima Rd.
Whittier, CA 90603
www.thewholechild.info
562-692-0383

SAN FERNANDO VALLEY

Aegis Treatment Centers
7246 Remmet Avenue
Canoga Park, CA 91303
818-206-0360

Associated Psychological Services
18546 Sherman Way, Ste. 202
Reseda, CA 91335
818-342-5868

Behavioral Management Group Inc.
8448 Reseda Blvd., Ste. 203
Northridge, CA 91324
www.bmgprograms.com
818-718-7100

Bridges
6267 Variel Ave., Ste. B
Woodland Hills, CA 91367
www.bridgesrehab.org
818-657-0411 x 210

Center for Individual and Family Counseling
5445 Laurel Canyon Blvd.
North Hollywood, CA 91607
www.cifc1.org
818-761-2227

Center for the Prevention of Family Violence
Behavioral Management Group Inc.
8448 Reseda Blvd., Ste. 203
Northridge, CA 91324
www.bmgprograms.com
818-718-7100

Center for the Prevention of Family Violence
21044 Sherman Way, Ste. 234
Canoga Park, CA 91303
www.preventionoffamilyviolence.com
818-883-2132

Child Development Institute- Canoga Park
7260 Owensmouth Ave.
Canoga Park, CA 91303

Appendix A

www.cdikids.org
818-712-0453

Child Development Institute- Woodland Hills
6340 Variel Ave., Ste. A
Woodland Hills, CA 91367
www.cdikids.org
818-888-4559

Child and Family Guidance Center
9650 Zelzah Ave.
Northridge, CA 91325
www.childguidance.org
818-993-9311

Children of the Night Inc.
14530 Sylvan St.
Van Nuys, CA 91411
www.childrenofthenight.org
818-908-4470

Clinical Counseling Associates
4419 Van Nuys Blvd., Ste. 307
Sherman Oaks, CA 91403
818-986-1161

Community Alcohol/Drug Treatment Foundation
15015 Oxnard St.
Van Nuys, CA 91411
818-787-4151

Community Psychological Services
16055 Ventura Blvd., Ste. 728
Encino, CA 91436

www.affordabletherapyla.com
818-907-7974

Counseling 4 Kids
601 S. Glenoaks Blvd., Ste. 200
Burbank, CA 91502
www.counseling4kids.org
818-441-7800

Counseling West
4419 Van Nuys Blvd., Ste. 310
Sherman Oaks, CA 91403
www.counselingwest.com
818-990-9898

CRI-Help, Inc.
11027 Burbank Blvd.
North Hollywood, CA 91601
www.cri-help.org
800-413-7660

Enki Health and Research Systems
150 E. Olive St., Ste. 203
Burbank, CA 91502
www.ehrs.com
866-227-1302

Friends of the Family
16861 Parthenia St.
North Hills, CA 91343
www.fofca.org/
818-988-4430

Appendix A

Five Star Counseling and Educational Services
6205 Laurel Canyon Blvd.
North Hollywood, CA 91606
818-763-6615

Life Counseling Center
10653 Riverside Dr.
North Hollywood, CA 91602
818-760-0074

New Directions for Youth
7315 N. Lankershim Blvd.
North Hollywood, CA 91605
www.ndfy.org
818-503-6330

Northridge Hospital Medical Center
18300 Roscoe Blvd.
Northridge, CA 91328
www.DignityHealth.org/NorthridgeHospital
818-885-5484 (Mental Health Crises Hotline)

Pacific Youth Lodge Services
4900 Serrania Ave.
Woodland Hills, CA 91364
www.plys.org
818-347-1577

Pepperdine Community Counseling Center
16830 Ventura Blvd., Ste. 216
Encino, CA 91436
www.gsep.pepperdine.edu
818-501-1678

Phillips Graduate Institute-Counseling Center
19900 Plummer St.
Chatsworth, CA 91311
www.pgi.edu
818-386-5615

Ranch San Antonio
21000 Plummer St.
Chatsworth, CA 91311
www.ranchosanantonio.org
818-882-6400

SFVMCH- MacDonald Carey East Valley
Mental Health
11631 Victory Blvd., Ste. 203
North Hollywood, CA 91606
www.movinglivesforward.org
818-908-3855

San Fernando Valley Counseling Center
8350 Reseda Blvd.
Northridge, CA 91324
www.sfvcc.org
818-341-1111 x382

Tarzana Treatment Centers
18646 Oxnard St.
Tarzana, CA 91356
www.tarzanatc.org
800-996-1051

Village Family Services
6736 Laurel Canyon Blvd., Ste. 200
North Hollywood, CA 91606

www.thevillagefs.org
818-755-8786

Valley Community Treatment Center
22110 Roscoe Blvd., Ste. 204
Canoga Park, CA 91304
www.vctreatment.org
818-713-8686

Valley Trauma Center
8700 Reseda Blvd., Ste. 209
Northridge, CA 91324
www.valleytrauma.org
818-886-0453

Wise and Healthy Agency
8374 Topanga Canyon Blvd., Ste. 209
Canoga Park, CA 91304
www.wiseandhealthyaging.org
818-444-0315

SAN GABRIEL VALLEY

Andrew Escajeda Comprehensive Care Services
1845 N. Fair Oaks Ave.
Pasadena, CA 91103
www.ci.pasadena.ca.us
626-744-6140

Center for Integrated Family and Health Services-The Family Center
540 S. Eremland Ave.
Covina, CA 91723
626-858-3315

East San Gabriel Valley Coalition for the Homeless
1345 Turnbull Canyon Rd.
Hacienda Heights, CA 91745
626-333-7260

Foothill Family Service
118 S. Oak Knoll Ave.
Pasadena, CA 91101
www.foothillfamily.org
626-993-3000

Grandview Foundation
225 Grandview St.
Pasadena, CA 91104
www. Grandviewfoundation.com
626-797-1124

Hathaway-Sycamores
210 S. DeLacy Ave., Suite 110
Pasadena, CA 91105
626-395-7100

Hillsides
940 Avenue 64
Pasadena, CA 91105
www.hillsides.org
323-254-2274

Hillsides
13001 Ramona Blvd.
Baldwin Park, CA 91706
626-373-2900

Maryvale (Residential Treatment for Girls)
7600 Graves Avenue
Rosemead, CA 91770
626-280-6510

Optimist Youth Homes & Family Services
6957 N. Figueroa St
Los Angeles, CA 90041
323-443-3175

Pasadena Senior Center
85 E. Holly St.
Pasadena, CA 91103
www.pasadenaseniorcenter.org
626-795-4331

Pacific Clinics
66 Hurlbut St.
Pasadena, CA 91105
www.pacificclinics.org
877-722-2737

Parents Anonymous Inc.
250 W. First St., Ste. 250
Claremont, CA 91711
Main phone: 909-621-6184 250
Hotline/Talk line/Warm line: 855-427-2736

Pasadena Council on Alcoholism and Drug Dependence
1245 E. Walnut Ave., Ste. 117
Pasadena, CA 91106
www.socialmodel.com
626-795-9127

Pasadena Mental Health Center
1495 N. Lake Ave.
Pasadena, CA 91104
www.pmhc.org
626-798-0907

Peace Over Violence (Sexual Assault Counseling)
892 N. Fair Oaks Ave., Ste. D
Pasadena, CA 91103
www.peaceoverviolence.org
626-584-6191

Rickman Recovery Center
1433 E. Route 66, Ste. F
Glendora, CA 91740
www.rickmanrecoverycenters.com
626-962-3203

Right to Life League of Southern California
5626 N. Rosemead Blvd.
Temple City, CA 91780
www.phc-sgv.org
626-309-0788

Rose City Center
595 E. Colorado Blvd., Ste. 418
Pasadena, CA 91101
www.rosecitycenter.org
626-793-8609

Rosemary Children's Services
36 South Kinneloa Ave #200
Pasadena, CA 91107
626-844-3033

Santa Anita Family Counseling Service
605 S. Myrtle Ave.
Monrovia, CA 91016
626-359-9358

Spiritt Family Services
2000 S. Tyler Ave.
South El Monte, CA 91733
www.spiritt.org
626-442-1400

Union Station Homeless Services
130 N. Marengo Ave.
Pasadena, CA 91101
www.unionstationhs.org
626-791-6610

Villa Esperanza Services
1757 N. Lake Ave.
Pasadena, CA 91104
www.villaesperanzaservices.org
626-398-4435

Verdugo Mental Health Center
1540 East Colorado Street
Glendale, CA 91205
818-244-7257

Westminster Center
867 E. Atchison St.
Pasadena, CA 91104
www.westminstercenter.org
626-798-0915

West San Gabriel Valley SELPA
15 W. Alhambra Rd.
Alhambra, CA 91801
www.wsgvselpa.org
626-943-3435

SANTA CLARITA VALLEY

American Health Services- El Dorado
26460 Summit Circle
Santa Clarita, CA 91350
www.americanhealthservices.org
877-557-7826

Hathaway-Sycamores
12510 Van Nuys Blvd.
Pacoima, CA 91331
www.hathaway-sycamores.org
818-896-8366

Hillview Mental Health Center
12408 Van Nuys Blvd.
Pacoima, CA 91331
www.hillviewmhc.org
818-896-1161

El Centro De Amistad- Canoga Park
566 S. Brand Blvd.
San Fernando, CA 91340
www.ecda.org
818-898-0223

El Nido Family Centers
10200 Sepulveda Blvd., Ste. 350

Mission Hills, CA 91345
818-830-3646

LACDMH- Santa Clarita Valley
23501 Cinema Dr., Ste. 210
Valencia, CA 91355
dmh.lacounty.gov
661-288-4800

Strength United
28231 Avenue Crocker, Ste. 30
Valencia, CA 91355
www.strengthunited.org
661-253-0258

SFV Community Mental Health Center
11565 Laurel Canyon Blvd., Ste. 101
Mission Hills, CA 91340
www.movinglivesforward.org
818-838-1352

SOUTH BAY

Airport Marina Counseling Services
7891 La Tijera Boulevard
Los Angeles, CA 90045
310- 670-1410

Champion Counseling Center
333 W. Florence Avenue
Inglewood, CA 90301
310-330-8000 x 3253

Counseling 4 Kids
19701 Hamilton Ave., Ste. 160
Torrance, CA 90502
www.counseling4kids.org
310-817-2177

Del Amo Behavioral Health System of Southern California
23700 Camino del Sol
Torrance, CA 90505
www.delamotreatment.com
310-530-1151

Children's Bureau
460 E. Carson Plaza Dr., Ste. 122
Carson, CA 90746
www.all4kids.org
310-523-9500

Children's Institute
21810 Normandie Ave.
Torrance, CA 90502
www.childrensinstitute.org
310-783-4677

Didi Hirsch
1328 W. Manchester Ave.
Los Angeles, CA 90044
www.didihirsch.org
323-778-9535

Emotional Change, Inc.
(Victim of Crime/Witness Counseling)
21151 S. Western Ave., Ste. 126A
Torrance, CA 90501

www.e-MotionalChange.com
323-256-9906

Guidance Center-San Pedro
222 W. 6th St., Ste. 230
San Pedro, CA 90731
www.tgclb.org
310-833-3135

Harbor View House
921 S. Beacon St.
San Pedro, CA 90731
www.healthview.org
310-547-3341 x361

LAC DMH
1000 W. Carson St.
Torrance, CA 90509
800-854-7771

Masada Homes (Adolescents)
108 W. Victoria St.
Gardena, CA 90248
www.masadahomes.org
310-715-2020

Neighborhood Family Center (Domestic Violence)
2309 E. Torrance Blvd., #201
Torrance, CA 90501
310-715-8885

Office of Samoan Affairs
20715 S. Avalon Blvd., #200
Carson, CA 90746

www.samoanaffairs.org
310-538-0555

Project ABC
21810 Normandie Ave.
Torrance, CA 90502
www.projectabc-la.org
855-436-1136

South Bay Center for Counseling
540 N. Marine Ave.
Wilmington, CA 90744
www.sbcc-la.org
310-414-2090

South Bay Children's Health Center
1617 Cravens Ave.
Torrance, CA 90501
www.sbchc.com
310-328-0855

STAR View Adolescent Center
4025 West 226th Street
Torrance, CA 90505
310-373-4556

WESTSIDE

Alafia Mental Health
3756 Santa Rosalia Dr., Ste. 628
Los Angeles, CA 90008
www.cihssinc.org
323-293-8771

Aviva Family and Children's Services
7120 Franklin Ave.
Los Angeles, CA 90046
www.avivacenter.org
323-876-0550

Centro De Ninos Y Padres
5151 State University Dr.
Los Angeles, CA 90032
www.centrodeninos.org
323-343-4420

Didi Hirsch Mental Health Services
4760 S. Sepulveda Blvd.
Culver City, CA 90230
www.didihirsch.org
310-390-6612

Edelman Westside Mental Health Center
11080 West Olympic Blvd
Los Angeles, CA 90064
310-966-6500

Family Service of Santa Monica
1533 Euclid Street
Santa Monica, CA 90404
310-451-9747

Help Group-Child and Family Center
12099 W. Washington Blvd.
Los Angeles, CA 90066
www.thehelpgroup.org
310-313-2595

Heritage Clinic-Mid City
155 N. Occidental Blvd., Ste. 243
Los Angeles, CA 90026
www.centerforagingresources.org
213-382-4400

Los Angeles Wings of Faith
2723 W. 54th St.
Los Angeles, CA 90043
www.resourcesunlimited.us
323-449-1300

Plaza Community Services
4018 City Terrace Dr.
Los Angeles, CA 90063
www.plazacs.org
323-268-3219

Saint Joseph Center
204 Hampton Drive
Venice, CA 90291
310-396-6468

Shields for Families, Inc.
215 S. Acacia Ave.
Compton, CA 90220
www.shieldsforfamilies.org
310-605-1777

St. Joseph Center
204 Hampton Dr.
Venice, CA 90291
www.stjosephctr.org
310-396-6468

Appendix A

Vista Del Mar Child and Family Services
3200 Motor Avenue
Los Angeles, CA 90034
310-836-1223

Westside Children's Center
5721 W. Slauson Ave., Suite 140
Culver City, CA 90230
www.westsidechildren.org
310-846-4100

APPENDIX B

Excerpt from *The Role of the Black Church in Serving the Psychological Needs of its Congregants: A Crises Intervention Manual, Protocols and Resources for Clergy*

Valinda M. Bowens, Psy.D.

I wanted to share the original reason for the creation of this manual. I hope you are enlightened by the following information.

In the African-American community, there is a stigma related to the function and necessity of mental health services. Due to many socio-historical and cultural influences, many African Americans have underutilized formal psychological services and relied on the Black Church and clergy, familial support, and social communities to satisfy their therapeutic needs.[49,50,51,52] Further, African Americans, when compared to other ethnic/racial groups in the United States, have more frequently utilized religious coping in place of formal mental health treatment.[53] Thus, collaborative relationships with the Black Church, through the use of Church-based health promotion programs, may help to reach underserved and vulnerable populations.

Historically and currently, mental illness and seeking formal psychological treatment has been stigmatized in the African-American community. According to the National Alliance on Mental Illness,[54] many factors have contributed to the underutilization of mental services. Socio-historical factors and barriers to treatment have included lack of trust, misdiagnosis, lack of access to care, quality of care, lack of knowledge, and stigma.[55,56,57] As a result, many African Americans have turned to non-traditional community supports, such as the Black Church, clergy, and familial and social networks to meet their therapeutic needs (Oubre, 2004).

The Black Church is the oldest, most respected, and highly influential institution founded, maintained, and controlled by African Americans.[58] Referred to as "the pulse of the African American community,"[59] the Black Church has not only met the religious needs of the community, but has fulfilled the social, political, educational, and psychological needs of the parishioners as well. Viewed through a community psychology lens, the Black Church has played a key role in the development of intervention and prevention programs, and has worked to bring awareness—to both parishioners and the larger community—to a variety of issues. Given the trust between the Black Church and the community, and the stigma associated with utilizing traditional mental health services, many African Americans have employed religious coping skills when dealing with psychological issues.[60]

African Americans, in comparison to other racial/ethnic groups, have utilized religious coping efforts more often during times of hardship and when faced with serious personal problems.[61] Many African Americans have used religious coping, as it provides a sense of hope, support, increased self-esteem, guidance, strength, and satisfaction as demonstrated through faith in God.[62] Researchers have also found that the Black Church meets the therapeutic needs of its parishioners through providing a place of belonging and by facilitating positive, cognitive, behavioral, and affective outcomes for members.[63]

In the African-American community, clergy play an important role as counselor and advisor, and they have repeatedly been sought out for counsel more often than formally trained mental health professionals when dealing with psychological problems, marital and family conflict, emotional adjustment issues, bereavement, substance abuse issues, unemployment, legal issues, and a host of other personal and psychological problems.[64,65,66] Because of the level of respect given to clergy in the African-American community, no cost to low cost of services, and the level of trust of clergy and the Black Church, many parishioners may not seek further medical or mental health treatment, although it may be necessary.[67]

Although clergy are depended on for many counseling needs, there is a lack of formal training among clergy that would better equip them to deal with the diversity and intensity of parishioner and community psychological needs.[68,69] Researchers have found that many members of the clergy may be unfamiliar with symptoms of psychopathology, may not recognize suicidal ideation, and may underestimate the severity of psychotic problems.[70] Further, some members of the clergy may also share some of the cultural and community stigma related to mental health, and may fear dealing with congregants who suffer from severe mental health issues.[71]

As the health disparity among racial/ethnic groups increases, the need to reach underserved populations is vitally important. Thus, the development and implementation of Church-based health promotion programs has been said to help reach marginalized populations and potentially reduce health disparities among groups.[72] Peterson, Atwood, and Yates[73] found that churches were willing to engage in health promotion programs, particularly those that promoted the integration of spiritual, mental, and physical health. Given their community focus, churches take into account all contextual factors and have an interest in providing holistic care. Therefore, collaboration with the Black Church can help to promote health and wellness, and offer a bridge between the African-American community and mental health awareness and treatment.[74,75,76]

There is extensive research on African Americans and their help-seeking and coping strategies. However, there has been less attention given to the integration of the Black Church and mental health, specifically the importance of the collaboration and implementation of Church-based mental health and counseling centers in urban African-American communities. To more fully understand the relationship between African Americans, mental health, and the role of the Black Church, research must look at the interaction between the three, and the pivotal impact that Black Church-based health promotion will have on the community it serves. Developing resources in the Black Church that promote psychological awareness, prevention, and wellness can help to reach underserved and marginalized African-American communities.

ENDNOTES

1. Middlebrook, D. (2012). Pastoral confidentiality: An ethical and legal responsibility. Enrichment Journal. Retrieved from http://enrichmentjournal.ag.org/201002/ejonline_201002_Pastor_Confid_.cfm
2. Suicide statistics. American Foundation for Suicide Prevention Web site. Updated 2017. Retrieved March 2, 2017 from http://afsp.org/
3. California Department of Mental Health, Office of Suicide Prevention: Fact Sheet. Updated 2014. Retrieved December 2014 from http://www.dhcs.ca.gov/services/MH/Documents/DMHOfficeofSuicidePreventionFactSheet.pdf
4. Ibid.
5. Suicide Prevention Resource Center, & Rodgers, P. (2011). *Understanding risk and protective factors for suicide: A primer for preventing suicide.* Newton, MA: Education Development Center, Inc.
6. Ibid.
7. Suicide prevention. How to help someone who is suicidal. HelpGuide.org Web site. Updated May 2016. Retrieved May 1, 2016 from http://www.helpguide.org/articles/suicide-prevention/suicide-prevention-helping-someone-who-is-suicidal.htm
8. Bryan, C., Steiner-Pappalardo, N., & Rudd, M. D. (2009). Exposure to a mnemonic interferes with recall of suicide warning signs in a community-based suicide prevention program. *Suicide and Life-Threatening Behavior.* 39:194-203.
9. *Diagnostic and Statistical Manual of Mental Disorders, Fifth Edition.* (2013). Arlington, VA: American Psychiatric Association.
10. Suicide Prevention Resource Center, & Rodgers, P. (2011). *Understanding risk and protective factors for suicide: A primer for preventing suicide.* Newton, MA: Education Development Center, Inc.
11. Comer, R. (2011). *Fundamentals of Abnormal Psychology.* 6th ed. New York, NY: Worth Publishers.

12. Kroenke, K., Spitzer, R., & Williams, J. B. (2001, September). The PHQ-9: validity of a brief depression severity measure. *J Gen Intern Med.* 16(9):606-13.
13. Bipolar Disorder. National Alliance on Mental Health Web site. Updated 2016. Retrieved April 3, 2016 from https://www.nami.org/Learn-More/Mental-Health-Conditions/Bipolar-Disorder
14. Kroenke K., Spitzer R., & Williams, J. B. (2001, September). The PHQ-9: validity of a brief depression severity measure. *J Gen Intern Med.* 16(9):606-13.
15. Ibid.
16. *Diagnostic and Statistical Manual of Mental Disorders, Fifth Edition.* (2013). Arlington, VA: American Psychiatric Association.
17. National Statistics. (2016). National Coalition Against Domestic Violence Web site. Retrieved December 2016 from http://www.ncadv.org/learn/statistics
18. What is Domestic Violence? Los Angeles Police Department Web site. Retrieved December 2014 from http://www.lapdonline.org/domestic_violence/content_basic_view/8853
19. Culross P. L., Fischer K., & Bedair, D. *Los Angeles County Domestic Violence Data Sources.* Los Angeles, CA: Los Angeles County Department of Public Health. Updated April 2010. Retrieved December 2014 from http://publichealth.lacounty.gov/ivpp/pdf_reports/DV%20Report/LA%20County%20Domestic%20Violence%20Data%20Sources%208.25.10.pdf
20. The Duluth Model Power and Control Wheel. Domestic Abuse Intervention Programs Web site. Updated 1984. Retrieved December 2014 from http://www.theduluthmodel.org/training/resources.html
21. Ibid.
22. California Partnership to End Domestic Violence. California domestic violence fact sheet. Updated 2011. Retrieved December 2014 from http://ywcasgv.org/DV_Fact_Sheet_2011.pdf
23. Ibid.
24. Martin G. What can pastors do to help victims of domestic violence in the church? *Assemblies of God Enrichment Journal.* Retrieved December 2014 from http://enrichmentjournal.ag.org/200704/200704_122_DomViolence.cfm

25. Murphy N. (2003). *God's reconciling love: A pastor's handbook on domestic violence*. Seattle, WA: FaithTrust Institute.
26. Miles A. (2000). *Domestic violence: What every pastor needs to know*. Minneapolis, MN: Augsburg Fortress.
27. Center for Behavioral Health Statistics and Quality. (2015). *Behavioral health trends in the United States: Results from the 2014 National Survey on Drug Use and Health* (HHS Publication No. SMA 15-4927, NSDUH Series H-50). Retrieved from http://www.samhsa.gov/ data/
28. Ibid.
29. University of California, Los Angeles Integrated Substance Abuse Programs. (2010). *Substance abuse and crime prevention act fiscal years 2008-2009 and 2009-2010 report*. Retrieved from http://publichealth.lacounty.gov/sapc/prop36/annualreport/SACPAReportFY2008-2010.pdf
30. Brecht M. (2013). *Drug Abuse Patterns and Trends in Los Angeles County, California: June 2013*. Bethesda, MD: National Institute on Drug Abuse. Updated November 2013. Retrieved December 2014 from https://www.drugabuse.gov/about-nida/organization/workgroups-interest-groups-consortia/community-epidemiology-work-group-cewg/trends-in-los-angeles-county-california
31. *Diagnostic and Statistical Manual of Mental Disorders, Fifth Edition*. (2013). Arlington, VA: American Psychiatric Association.
32. Apthorp S. (1985). *Alcohol and substance abuse: A clergy handbook*. New York, NY: Morehouse-Barlow.
33. Gostin L. (1976). Tarasoff v. Regents of the University of California. In: Gostin L. (Ed.) (2002). *Public Law and Ethics: A Reader*. Berkley, CA: University of California Press.
34. Ewing, C. P. (2005). Tarasoff reconsidered. *American Psychological Association Judicial Notebook*. 36(7):112. Retrieved January 5, 2015 from http://www.apa.org/monitor/julaug05/jn.aspx
35. Herman M. (2009). The liability of clergy for acts of their congregants. *The Georgetown Law Journal*. 98(153):153-184. Retrieved January 5, 2014 from http://georgetownlawjournal.org/files/pdf/98-1/Herman.PDF
36. Schaefer, A., & Levine, D. No sanctuary from the law: Legal issues facing clergy. *Loy. L.A. L. Rev*. 177. Retrieved January 5, 2015 from http://

37. digitalcommons.lmu.edu/cgi/viewcontent.cgi?article=2021&context=llr
37. Herman M. (2009). The liability of clergy for acts of their congregants. *The Georgetown Law Journal.* 98(153):153-184. Retrieved January 5, 2014 from http://georgetownlawjournal.org/files/pdf/98-1/Herman.PDF
38. Ibid.
39. Merrill, G. (2013). Assessing client dangerousness to self and others: Stratified risk management approaches. *Berkeley Social Welfare.* Retrieved January 6, 2015 from http://socialwelfare.berkeley.edu/sites/default/files/users/gregmerrill/Assessing%20client%20dangerousness%20to%20self%20and%20others,%20stratified%20risk%20management%20approaches,%20Fall%202013.pdf
40. Child Abuse Statistics and Facts. Child Help Web site. Updated 2014. Retrieved June 2016 from https://www.childhelp.org/child-abuse-statistics/
41. Los Angeles County Department of Children and Family Services (2017). 2015-2016 DCFS Biennial Report. Retrieved March 2, 2017 from http://dcfs.lacounty.gov/Release/2015-2016BiennialReport_r2.pdf
42. Child Welfare Information Gateway. Clergy as Mandated Reporters of Child Abuse and Neglect. Retrieved January 6, 2015 from https://www.childwelfare.gov/pubPDFs/clergymandated.pdf
43. Child Abuse and Neglect Reporting Act. Cal. Penal Code § 11166 et. seq.
44. Child Abuse Mandated Reported Training California. California Department of Social Services Web site. Updated 2011. Retrieved November 2014 from http://mandatedreporterca.com/training/clergy.htm
45. Donner M. (2008). Mandated Reporting of Suspected Child Abuse. *Board of Psychology.* Retrieved July 7, 2016 from http://c.ymcdn.com/sites/www.cpapsych.org/resource/resmgr/imported/files/ethics/Donner(2008)Mandated%20Reporting%20of%20Child%20Abuse.pdf
46. Ibid.
47. Ibid.
48. Ibid.
49. Barnes S. (2005). Black church culture and community Action. *Social Forces.* Retrieved from file:///D:/Dissertation/Black%20Church%20Articles/Barnes%202005%20Black%20Church%20Culture%20&%20Community%20Action.pdf

50. Sanders, R. (2002). The Black church: Bridge over troubled water. In Sanders, J. L., & Bradley, C. (Eds.), *Counseling African American families* (pp. 73-84). Alexandria, VA: American Counseling Association.
51. Thompson, D. A., & McRae, M. B. (2001). The need to belong: A theory of the therapeutic function of the Black church tradition. *Counseling and Values. 46*:40-53. doi:10.1002/j.2161-007X.2001.tb00205.x
52. Williams, S. D. (2008). *The impact of the Black church on Black women's sense of self.* (Doctoral Dissertation). Available from ProQuest Dissertations and Theses.
53. Oubre, A. (2004). *Exploring emotional intimacy among African American female survivors of childhood sexual abuse who utilize Black Church support services.* (Doctoral dissertation). Seaton Hall University, South Orange Village, New Jersey. (UMI No. 3156500).
54. Diala, C., Muntaner, C., Walwarth, C., Nickerson, K. J., LaVeist, T. A., & Leaf, P. J. (2000). Racial differences in attitudes toward professional mental health care and in the use of services. *Journal of Orthopsychiatry, 70*(4):455-464. doi:10.1037/h0087736
55. Holden, K. B., & Xanthos, C. (2009). Disadvantages in mental health care among African Americans. *Journal of Health Care for the Poor and Underserved. 20*:17-23. doi:10.1037/a0038122
56. Obasi, E. M., & Leong, F. T. (2009). Psychological distress, acculturation, and mental health-seeking attitudes among people of African descent in the United States: A preliminary investigation. *Journal of Counseling Psychology. 56*(2):227-238. doi:10.1037/a0014865
57. Adkison-Bradley, C., Johnson, D., Lipford-Sanders, J., Duncan, L., & Holcomb-McCoy, C. (2005). Forging a collaborative relationship between the Black Church and the counseling profession. *Counseling and Values. 49*:147-154. doi:10.1002/j.2161-007X.2005.tb00261.x
58. Lewis-Coles, M. E. L., & Constantine, M. G. (2006). Racism-related stress, Africultural coping, and religious problem-solving among African Americans. *Cultural Diversity and Ethnic Minority Psychology. 12*(3):433-443. doi:10.1037/1099-9809.12.3.433
59. Ibid.

60. Oubre, A. (2004). *Exploring emotional intimacy among African American female survivors of childhood sexual abuse who utilize Black Church support services.* (Doctoral dissertation). Seaton Hall University, South Orange Village, New Jersey. (UMI No. 3156500).

61. Hendricks, L., Bore, S., & Waller, L. (2012). An examination of spirituality in the African American church. *National Forum of Multicultural Issues Journal.* 9(1):1-8.

62. Shipp, M. E. (2009). *Psychological factors related to African American clergy and clergy family's help-seeking attitudes.* (Doctoral dissertation). Alliant International University at Los Angeles, Alhambra, CA. (3421107)

63. Thompson, D. A., & McRae, M. B. (2001). The need to belong: A theory of the therapeutic function of the Black church tradition. *Counseling and Values.* 46:40-53. doi:10.1002/j.2161-007X.2001.tb00205.x

64. Taylor, R. J., Ellison, C. G., Chatters, L. M., Levin, J. S., & Lincoln, K. D. (2000). Mental health services in faith communities: The role of clergy in Black churches. *National Association of Social Workers.* 45(1):73-87. doi:10.1093/sw/45.1.73

65. National Alliance on Mental Illness. (2013). *Mental illness facts and numbers.* Retrieved from http://www.nami.org/factsheets/mentalillness_factsheet.pdf

66. Thompson, D. A., & McRae, M. B. (2001). The need to belong: A theory of the therapeutic function of the Black church tradition. *Counseling and Values.* 46:40-53. doi:10.1002/j.2161-007X.2001.tb00205.x

67. Diala, C., Muntaner, C., Walwarth, C., Nickerson, K. J., LaVeist, T. A., & Leaf, P. J. (2000). Racial differences in attitudes toward professional mental health care and in the use of services. *Journal of Orthopsychiatry.* 70(4):455-464. doi:10.1037/h0087736

68. Leavey, G., Lowenthal, K., & King, M. (2007). Challenges to sanctuary: The clergy as a resource for mental health care in the community. *Social Science and Medicine.* 65:548-559. doi:10.1016/j.socscimed.2007.03.050

69. Taylor, R. J., Ellison, C. G., Chatters, L. M., Levin, J. S., & Lincoln, K. D. (2000). Mental health services in faith communities: The role of clergy in Black churches. *National Association of Social Workers.* 45(1):73-87. doi:10.1093/sw/45.1.73

70. National Alliance on Mental Illness. (2013). *Mental illness facts and numbers.* Retrieved from http://www.nami.org/factsheets/mentalillness_factsheet.pdf
71. Leavey, G., Lowenthal, K., & King, M. (2007). Challenges to sanctuary: The clergy as a resource for mental health care in the community. *Social Science and Medicine.* 65:548-559. doi:10.1016/j.socscimed.2007.03.050
72. Campbell, M. K., Hudson, M. A., Resnicow, K., Blakeney, N., Paxton, A., & Baskin, M. (2007). Church-Based Health Promotion interventions: Evidence and lessons learned. *Annual Review of Public Health.* 28:213-234. doi:10.1146/annurev.publhealth.28.021406.144016
73. Peterson, J., Atwood, J. R., & Yates, B. (2002). Key elements for Church-Based Health Promotion programs: Outcome-based literature review. *Public Health Nursing.* 19(6):401-411. doi:10.1046/j.1525-1446.2002.19602.x
74. Campbell, M. K., Hudson, M. A., Resnicow, K., Blakeney, N., Paxton, A., & Baskin, M. (2007). Church-Based Health Promotion interventions: Evidence and lessons learned. *Annual Review of Public Health.* 28:213-234. doi:10.1146/annurev.publhealth.28.021406.144016
75. Carter-Edwards, L., Hooten, E. G., Bruce, M. A., Toms, F., Lloyd, C. L., & Ellison, C. (2012). Pilgrimage to wellness: An exploratory report of rural African American clergy perceptions of church health promotion capacity. *Journal of Prevention and Intervention in the Community.* 40(3):194-207. doi: 10.1080/10852352.2012.680411
76. Hankerson, S. H., & Weissman, M. M. (2012). Church-Based Health Programs for mental disorders among African Americans: A review. *Psychiatric Services.* 63(3):243-249. doi:10.1176/appi.ps.201100216

www.ingramcontent.com/pod-product-compliance
Lightning Source LLC
LaVergne TN
LVHW051559070426
835507LV00021B/2664